States
of Unconsciousness in Three Tales
by C. F. Meyer

States
of Unconsciousness
in Three Tales
by C. F. Meyer

Dennis McCort

Lewisburg
Bucknell University Press
London and Toronto: Associated University Presses

Associated University Presses
440 Forsgate Drive
Cranbury, NJ 08512

Associated University Presses
25 Sicilian Avenue
London WC1A 2QH, England

Associated University Presses
P.O. Box 488, Port Credit
Mississauga, Ontario
Canada L5G 4M2

The paper used in this publication meets the requirements
of the American National Standard for Permanence of Paper
for Printed Library Materials Z39.48-1984.

Library of Congress Cataloging-in-Publication Data

McCort, Dennis.
  States of unconsciousness in three tales.

  Bibliography: p.
  Includes index.
  1. Meyer, Conrad Ferdinand, 1825–1898—Criticism
and interpretation.   2. Subconsciousness in literature.
I. Title.
PT2432.Z9M34   1988   833′.7   87-47786
ISBN 0–8387–5130–X (alk. paper)

Printed in the United States of America

For Dorothy

Contents

*States
of Unconsciousness in Three Tales
by C. F. Meyer*

Introduction

CONRAD FERDINAND MEYER is well known as an artist who never ceased to be beguiled by the phenomenon of hiddenness. Things gained in interest and importance for him as they became less accessible to ordinary observation or public scrutiny. There is more than a seed of authorial self-disclosure in Hans the Bowman's eavesdropping on Becket during the latter's hour of anguished meditation or Gustel Leubelfing's peeping through a crack in the wall in order to listen in on that confidential exchange between Gustavus Adolphus and Wallenstein. So often has Meyer been characterized as a habitué of the covert: an example from the older critical literature would be Louis Wiesmann's fine book, *Conrad Ferdinand Meyer, der Dichter des Todes und der Maske;* one from the more recent wave of studies would be the eighth chapter of Marianne Burkhard's *Conrad Ferdinand Meyer,* entitled "The Hidden Wound."

The other side of this coin is frustration. Meyer was terribly frustrated by the conviction that the truth of people and events—and hence their power—always lay just beyond the sphere of his own direct perception. What a paltry instrument indeed must be a mind that can never embrace without impediment the things it intuitively holds in greatest awe: God, spirit, history, the wellsprings of human behavior. Certainly Meyer felt his own power as a creative artist to be beyond his ken. (Of course, he had the good sense not to be too troubled by this.) On his best days he could display a kind of blind cosmological optimism, but he knew only too well that that optimism was blind. He could never quite get past his sense of disappointment that whatever force(s) might be guiding the world was unknown and probably unknowable. Thus in a letter to Friedrich von Wyβ: "So I tell myself that the same Master who has ordered this [the wondrous Alps] has surely also drawn His lines, though they be for me hidden, in the totally different area of history, lines which guide and coordinate the whole."[1] For Meyer the currents of essential reality were ultimately "hidden."

With grim resignation he bore his fate as a "son of the nineteenth century," for whom grand metaphysical first principles had become like so many ghosts dispersed by the sobering piecemeal truths of empirical science. Happily for us, however, those ghosts found their way into his fiction, recast there as fundamental levels of reality of which the hero or heroine is most often unconscious. This very unawareness of the inner workings of things that stamps Meyer's characters was an artist's unique way of turning a private psycho-spiritual liability into a public benefaction.

In these pages I will examine three tales in which the major characters are shown to be typically, chronically, and in two cases fatally unaware of a potent field of reality that constitutes the essential "world" of the work. It will be seen that the state of unconsciousness, variously cosmological or psychological, in which these characters live out their lives is the guiding principle of Meyer's art of characterization. Thus does Meyer confer a kind of apotheosis on the fact of hiddenness by dwelling on the phenomenon of unconsciousness, its subjective correlative.

The three tales at issue are *Das Amulett, Gustav Adolfs Page,* and *Das Leiden eines Knaben,* and one might identify the covert but fundamental level of reality in the world of each tale as history, psyche, and Eden, respectively. My discussion of *Das Amulett* focuses on the obliviousness of the characters to those contemporary historical forces by which they are shaped and which they in turn help to shape—hence, "historical uncon-sciousness." I attempt to show that the tale is, in effect, a narratization of Tolstoy's axiom that those who would understand history are condemned to sterility of action, while, conversely, those who "make" history are ignorant of its nature.

The middle section, which takes up the much-underrated novella *Gustav Adolfs Page,* analyzes the heroine's tragic military adventure as the predeter-mined outcome of unresolved unconscious conflicts rooted in childhood. My purpose is to show that Meyer has fashioned here a kind of proto-psychoanalytic Joan of Arc replete with Electra complex and perverted gender identity. I hasten to add, however, that all the psychology is implicit in the art of characterization, with never a trace of textbookishness—nor could there be, since the definitive textbook was yet to be written: Meyer penned his tale some eighteen years before the publication of Freud's land-mark *Interpretation of Dreams.* Indeed, Freud read Meyer during the late 1890s and acknowledges having learned from him. The last third of this section is an intellectual-historical sub-essay, showing how a constellation of pre-Freudian artists and thinkers—among others, Schopenhauer, Hartmann, Ludwig, Bachofen and Michelet—were generating the kinds of depth-psychological ideas that Freud would eventually assemble in his great system and that, in the case of *Gustav Adolfs Page,* ignited Meyer's genius for subtle psychological characterization. My analysis of the text of Meyer's story is close, even exacting, often dwelling on the salient detail of speech, gesture, or facial expression, as psychoanalysis itself does, but, I would hope, never losing sight of the overall shape of the narrative.

Rounding out my study is an exploration of what I perceive to be an elaborate subtext of myth that runs throughout *Das Leiden eines Knaben*. The myth in question is that of Eden and the Fall from Grace. Meyer's genius is here manifest in his brilliant use of the lapsarian myth to intimate the notion of unconsciousness as the fundamental fact of the human condition. Man's unconsciousness is the loss of his ability to *see*, the very ability that once kept him at one with nature. His original sin consists in his having turned his power of sight in upon himself so that his entire experience is now cripplingly self-referential. Fallen man is self-conscious man, and self-conscious man engages not in seeing, but in "seenness," its perverse antithesis. He is forever experiencing himself as seen by "the other," be that other real, imagined, or even an alienated part of himself. Man's vaunted self-awareness thus amounts to a loss of spiritual awareness or vision. Having lost his power of sight, which is the essence of Edenic experience and his link to fundamental reality, man is fitfully asleep in the smothering embrace of his own ego.

There has been a running debate of sorts in the critical literature on Meyer over the question of the author's possible fatalism.[2] Are Meyer's characters essentially puppets, reacting unawares to the manipulations of obscure forces, or are they free agents and therefore responsible for their actions? Even from the above cursory descriptions of my analyses, it must be evident to the reader that I stand with the fatalists—for the most part. I say "for the most part" because to me the issue is far from the black-and-white exercise in logic that Michael Shaw performs and George Reinhardt applauds in support of the voluntarist position.[3] Meyer was an artist, not a philosopher, so that the question is not whether his works comprise a systematic and consistent "argument" in favor of or against fatalism, but rather whether the *predominant* mode of his characters' behavior is free or deterministic. For it is only when regarded as a relative tendency, strong to one degree or another in this or that circumstance, and not as an absolute posture, that the fatalism question lends itself to useful discussion. Therefore, if I were asked my view of the matter, I would say that, at least in the three novellas treated in this study, the major characters behave in an identifiably deterministic way most of the time. Which is to imply that glimpses of freedom are also occasionally built into Meyer's fictive world—indeed, in *Das Leiden eines Knaben* the glimpse becomes a pellucid vision of man's limitless potential for freedom. Freedom and fatalism—or determinism, in its nineteenth-century nomenclature—generally occur in varying admixtures in Meyer's fictive world, with the latter as the clearly dominant strain. They are like two discontinuous and yet somehow strangely intimate psycho-spiritual orders, determinism being man's common lot, freedom his remote possibility.

Only in *Gustav Adolfs Page* does the absence of freedom strike one as total. One might even regard the character of Gustel Leubelfing as a particularly apt prefiguration of Freud's gloomy pronouncement that "anatomy is destiny." However, what gives anatomy or gender its absolute power over Gustel's life is her very unawareness of her own painfully twisted relationship to it. What she does not know, that of which she is unconscious, does in truth kill her. In this tale it is psychological self-ignorance that constitutes man's essential bondage, this bondage a web so tangled that it would appear seamless.

In *Das Amulett* human behavior is shown to be the unconscious process through which history, as cosmic first principle, works out its own—to us—obscure ends. This is precisely the metaphysical insight vouchsafed Schadau during his dark night of incarceration in the Louvre. Here at least one can point to a Meyerian scene in which freedom, in the sense of a character's emancipation from the narrow focus of his own cultural conditioning, would appear to be possible for man. But the freedom Meyer the creator gives his hero with one hand, he takes away with the other. Schadau's illumination lasts but a moment and leaves no discernible mellowing trace in his rigid Calvinist character. Moreover, even the quality of freedom implicit in the vision itself is specious, for its prerequisite is a bodiless state of consciousness, leaving its beneficiary impotent to act on the wisdom thus attained. In the world of *Das Amulett* history is either made or grasped, and the dichotomy remains unresolved.

Das Leiden eines Knaben is perhaps Meyer's most determined effort to shape a vision of human freedom in narrative terms. Through a largely oblique but consistent invocation of the myth of Eden, Meyer portrays Julian, Mouton, the latter's dog, and, to some extent, Fagon as a tiny utopia in the midst of the Sun King's "fallen" court society. When absorbed in painting, Mouton and Julian lose their sense of separateness from nature, that awareness of self as incontestably existing apart from the world, and merge with the visual field. Thus liberated from the shackles of ego through a process of totally uncluttered seeing, the Garden community awakens to its fundamental solidarity with all of creation, while all around it a syco-phantic aristocracy writhes in the throes of an enslaving self-consciousness. But there is trouble even in Paradise as Meyer brings the aesthetic power of doubt to bear on his theme: Julian, a mythical messianic figure come to save a corrupt society from itself through the sway of his simple goodness, is no match for the powerful ignorance of his spiritual inferiors and ends up instead falling prey himself to the Original Sin of seenness. He suffers the agony of humiliation, that inescapable liability of self-awareness, and dies pitifully in a paroxysmic craving for self-aggrandizement. *Das Leiden eines Knaben* presents freedom as a spiritual possibility, but no more than that. Its realization seems infinitely remote, for the world remains far too dark a place for the fragile, flickering light of Edenic consciousness.

What is arresting is not the deterministic hue of Meyer's view of human nature—by the late nineteenth century the deterministic perspective had become commonplace among the educated classes—but rather the enormous surge of creative power this grim conviction released in him. Truly he managed to turn lemons into lemonade. How amazing that he could so deftly allow that sense of doomed unawareness of the powers that be, which must have hovered about him throughout his life, to transmute and channel itself into a steady current of artistic activity. How amazing, in other words, that Meyer was able to use the very chains by which he felt bound, the chains of his own belief in the delusive nature of ordinary consciousness, as redemptive lifelines for hoisting himself up onto the expansive terrain of *Dichtung*. How amazing, indeed, that he could discover within the nimbus of his own incipient madness the bracing sanity of the muse.

It is just such an uplifting view of Meyer's motivation as an artist that I would offer as an antidote to the escapist image that has dogged the author for so long. Perhaps nowhere has the neoromantic image of Meyer as the "delicate child of life," driven by its Philistine crassness into the rarefied sanctuary of art (à la, say, Thomas Mann's Detlev Spinnell), been painted in stronger colors than in an article of 1940 by Arthur Burkhard, a scholar whose work on Meyer I otherwise admire. In the final pages of that article Burkhard bares what can only be called his contempt for Meyer, whom he brands a cowardly aesthete. Thus variously:

> Schiller struggles with life and tries to give it meaning and direction. Meyer, lacking Schiller's strength, self-confidence, and courage, and totally without Schiller's philosophical approach to life's problems, plays with life in a condescending and patronizing manner. . . . Too weak to master life as it meets him in himself and his times, . . . Meyer turns away from the exhilarating struggle with life as it is. . . . This timidity, masquerading as reserve, this weakness and resultant incapacity impart to Meyer's works a spirit of pessimism, hopelessness, and despair that is not always apparent to the casual reader. . . . Meyer . . . has no constructive solution to offer. Back of all phenomena there is a power, be it *Schicksal* or *Gott*, against which all struggle is of no avail. . . . [Meyer flees] to the past for its effect of calm and magnificence because of his dislike of reality and his fear of the present.[4]

While Burkhard and I are in agreement as to the predominantly deterministic nature of Meyer's fictive world, we take radically opposite views of the creative impulse generating that world. For Burkhard that impulse, stripped naked, is one of escape from reality; for me it is one of confrontation. Far from being a flight into an anesthetizing past, Meyer's historical fiction is precisely the arena he chose in which to confront a present reality experienced as bleak, that is, the reality of his own keenly felt inadequacy to the conditions of life within and without. What Burkhard deplores as weakness, the failure of the tales to offer a "constructive solution," I take to be the core of strength, aesthetic and moral, that pervades all of Meyer's work: the capacity to be choicelessly aware of his own tormenting anxiety, to be aware of it without yielding to the conditioned reflex to "fix" it, aware of it long enough and deeply enough to mine it profitably for literature. Faulting Meyer for not taking a lesson from Schiller is like scolding the melancholiac for not being sanguine or "the sick soul" for not being "healthy-minded."[5] It is to refuse to face the reality of the style as infallible fingerprint of the man, for the fact is that Meyer was roused by his pessimism to as legitimate an artistic enterprise as was Schiller by his optimism. The vitality of the work always hinges on the integrity of the artist's adherence to his own distinctive vision, whatever its emotional coloration. Moreover, if Burkhard (et al.) were right about Meyer's escapism, is it not odd that this world of the past to which the author supposedly flees "for its effect of calm" is, as Burkhard himself describes it, steeped in "pessimism, hopelessness, and despair"? One wonders just what sort of sedation Burkhard imagines Meyer to have enjoyed in conjuring up such a world.

On the contrary, I see Meyer as having endured considerable suffering in his brave and honest effort to recreate, in historical garb, the terrifying world of his own inner experience. His fiction illustrates the paradox of the coterminal relationship of freedom and determinism. His tales show how intensely the freest of human acts, that of artistic creation, can be stimulated by squarely facing the agony of one's own psychological bondage. Intuitively Meyer knew that the only way out of that agony, out of that bondage, led straight through it. The tales constitute just such a dark journey toward transcendence.

1

Historical Consciousness
versus Action in *Das Amulett*

ONE first encounters this rather rarefied theme of unconsciousness in what would seem a most unlikely place, for *Das Amulett* is arguably Meyer's most extroverted and melodramatic work of fiction. The artistry of the tale, the author's earliest, is indeed subtle, which may help to explain its gradual, at times grudging, recognition among critics. Deemed a triumph on publication for its integrity of plot structure,[1] the tale fell in the critical canon of our own century to the status of an apprenticeship exercise, faulted variously, even contradictorily, for its awkward organization, its strained symbolism, its hedging on questions of destiny versus free will, and its outright fatalism.[2] Sporadic attempts to rehabilitate the work,[3] from the mid-thirties through the late fifties, finally issued in a ground swell of positive revaluation in the late sixties and early seventies, a full century after its appearance.[4]

The irony of the critical picture as it now stands is that the contemporary critics who have taken a close look at the text of *Das Amulett* and found it meritorious are in no more agreement as to the source of that merit than were the earlier critics with regard to its defectiveness. The mind reels at the veritable Babel of interpretations. The confusion seems to revolve around a basic uncertainty over the light in which Meyer intends the reader to regard his Calvinist hero, Hans von Schadau. D. A. Jackson stresses "the distinction to be made between Schadau's [bigoted] mental consciousness and Meyer's own,"[5] and argues that "forty years after the massacre [of Saint Bartholomew's Day], Schadau is as blind as he was at the time. His creator Meyer has no love for him."[6] Gunter Hertling, on the other hand, tries to persuade us that Schadau does indeed outgrow his religious fanaticism and that Meyer is really portraying "the transformation of an orthodox Protestant into a tolerant man who shares in God's grace,"[7] replete with auto-biographical resonances. Consistent with this more charitable view of Schadau's character is Paul Schimmelpfennig's interpretation, according to which Schadau's spontaneous acts of generosity toward those proscribed by his faith—his uncommitted uncle, the old Catholic Boccard and the areligious Bohemian fencing-master—gradually undermine his narrow Calvinist precepts, ultimately enabling him, during the civil crisis, to "appeal to Boccard to help save Gasparde 'im Namen der Muttergottes von Einsiedeln,'" this last "a clear manifestation of heightened spiritual flexibility."[8] Finally, George Reinhardt takes a different tack completely, viewing Schadau and the novella as a whole, along with the lyric, "Die Karyatide," as Meyer's vehicles for an indictment of "French bloodlust as manifested by the Massacre of St. Bartholomew as well as by the excesses of the French Revolution and the Commune of 1871." Between the lines Reinhardt would have us detect Meyer's need to rationalize his own enthusiasm for the *Realpolitik* of the new *Reich*. Showing the French Catholics as demoniacally possessed fanatics "enables the moral absolutist in Meyer to accept the Franco-Prussian War as a Manichaean struggle between the armies of light and darkness."[9]

Reinhardt's political extrapolations show the interpretative extremes to which the puzzling character of Schadau can give rise. The question remains: How is one to take Meyer's hero? As reminiscing first-person narrator, is he essentially the same hardheaded partisan he was forty years ago; or have the atrocities he has lived through, committed by both sides in the name of religion, made him more aware of the mindless, mechanical nature of fanaticism? Any interpretation of *Das Amulett* hinges on the question of whether Schadau has learned from the experiences he relates to us. At the risk of compounding the confusion of critical voices, but also in hopes of resolving it, I venture here an interpretation of the novella centered on a scene that almost all the various readings acknowledge as revelatory of Meyer's intent, but that I believe has eluded correct interpretation up to now: Schadau's vision during his night of imprisonment in the Louvre. By closely examining this scene and its function within the novella's inner form, I intend to show that the meaning of *Das Amulett* as *literature* has little to do with pronouncements against religious bigotry—or any other moral issue—and everything to do with the portrayal of the characters' varied levels of historical consciousness in relation to their respective roles in contemporary events. My interpretation will then open up to a discussion of some of the intellectual issues surrounding Meyer's artistic conception and a general comment on the quality of realism in the novella that such a reading discloses.

The scene in question is brief: Boccard, whose loyalty to Schadau as a fellow Swiss overshadows their religious differences, has locked Schadau in his room in the Louvre to protect him from the impending massacre of the Huguenots. Schadau is unaware of his countryman's friendly motives and suspects him of betrayal. The shock of this imagined betrayal jolts Schadau into a crisis of doubt and panic. Perhaps the king has gone mad and turned against the Huguenots. Could his warm affection for Admiral Coligny have turned to bitter hatred within a few hours? Worried over these matters and over his unexplained lateness at home, where his new bride, Gasparde, waits for him, Schadau sees his darkest fears confirmed as he peers out through the bars of an elevated window at three sinister figures on a parapet just above him: King Charles, his brother, the Duke of Anjou, and Catherine de Medici, the queen mother. The first shot rings out, and Schadau witnesses Catherine's "benediction" of the massacre: " 'Finally!' the queen whispered, relieved. And the three figures of the night disappeared from the parapet."[10] Schadau's panic mounts to a fever pitch as he realizes his utter helplessness in a situation involving grave danger to his wife: "My hair stood on end. My blood froze in my veins" (1:67). Reduced to the desperate straits of a trapped animal, whose instincts of rage and fear merge in the single, all-consuming urge to escape, Schadau flails away at the heavy oaken door and the barred window, in vain.

In order to understand the true significance of the vision that Schadau is to have later during this agonized night of incarceration, one must take careful note of the distraught quality of his emotional state at this point, especially its physiological manifestations: "My hair stood on end. My blood froze in my veins. . . . A fevered chill seized me, and my teeth chattered against each other. Approaching insanity, I threw myself upon Boccard's bed and rolled back and forth in mortal fear" (1:67–68). Hair raised, blood curdling, chills, chattering teeth, convulsions, a sense of impending madness—these are the symptoms of a body operating on an emergency level and poised for survival action but to which every path of action has been blocked. Meyer does not present these physiological details simply as strokes of sensationalism to intensify the melodrama; rather, as will become apparent, they form an essential prelude to a mode of escape that Schadau would never have thought to attempt deliberately—escape from his own body into a sphere of meta-physical truth.

Curiously, Schadau, who is recording these events some forty years after their occurrence "to ease my mind in this way" (1:34), tells us nothing of the few hours between his convulsive mortal fear and this exosomatic deliverance. Perhaps the unnarrated interval, during which his consciousness could only have congealed into a numbed despair, is too painful to recall. It may also indicate a transitional nimbus between normal conscious awareness and the limpid breadth of vision to come. In any case, it yields along toward dawn to an event that defies all known natural law. Inexplicably, Schadau finds himself back up at the barred window. Peering through, he is witness to a dialogue on the folly of religious fanaticism carried on between the goddess of the Seine and a caryatid supporting the parapet just outside his room. There are several indications in the text that Schadau's experience of these extraordinary beings is not meant to be taken as merely a dream or gratuitous vision of the *deus-ex-machina* sort, but as an actual out-of-the-body experience (OOBE) leading to metaphysical insight.[11] This phenomenon, which is akin to satori, mystical release and similar ecstatic states of consciousness, is only gradually coming to be understood by psychologists; but OOBEs have been spontaneously happening to people both in life and in literature from time immemorial. Robert Crookall's landmark *Study and Practice of Astral Projection* contains hundreds of "accounts of people who claimed temporarily to leave the body, to be conscious apart from it, and to 'return' and recount their experiences."[12] Similarly, Charles Tart, in *States of Consciousness*, discusses "people [who] report existing at space/time locations different from that of their physical bodies, or being outside of space/time altogether."[13] Meyer provides sufficient clues to indicate that Schadau's perception of the caryatid and the river goddess occurs in just such a state of consciousness apart from his physical body. That Schadau's experience is not simply a dream or a vision but a bodiless waking state of expanded consciousness has important implications for Meyer's central purpose, which is to show the dichotomy within the major characters between historical awareness and decisive action.

One of the typical features of OOBEs is that they are only partially remembered or remembered as dreams.[14] In recalling his experience Schadau is hesitant to label it a dream, even though his reason has no other convenient category for it. He is intuitively aware of its uncanny nature, since he admits that he had drifted "into an indescribable condition between waking and napping" (1:68). This hypnagogic or twilight area of consciousness when one is no longer awake but not yet asleep is most conducive to the occurrence of an OOBE, especially when one is self-preoccupied and observing oneself" in the process of falling asleep."[15] Schadau is not merely self-preoccupied but obsessed with the desperate impotence of his incarceration. Unconsciously he is seeking the only way out of his prison that is left him. The complete frustration of a life-and-death need to get to another location can nudge the psychic body loose from its moorings in the physical body. Without explaining how he got there, since he himself does not know, he says simply: "I thought I was still clutching at the iron bars of the window and looking out upon the restlessly flowing Seine" (1:68). This is no dream, any more than his first glimpse through the barred window at the Machiavellian triumvirate had been earlier on. Dreams, even *Fieberträume*,[16] occur during sleep, and to assume Schadau capable of attaining sleep in his present predicament is to fly in the face of the most elementary logic of emotions. Moreover, as in reality, dreams in Meyer's fiction—witness Pfannenstiel's erotic dream in *Der Schuß von der Kanzel* or Leubelfing's guilt-ridden nightmares in *Gustav Adolfs Page*—are intimate expressions of a character's

deep-rooted wishes and fears. By contrast, Schadau's vision is oddly imper-
sonal; it strikes one as less psychological manifestation than metaphysical
revelation. And he is not directly involved in it at all, but simply witness to a
dialogue between two larger-than-life entities that take no notice of him.
One is led to conclude that Schadau's consciousness has left his body. While
his physical body remains on Boccard's bed in cataleptic stupor, the psychic
body in which his consciousness is now draped drifts up to the barred
window just beneath the ceiling. Ironically, the cell from which Schadau is
liberated is not the object of his violent protestations but the moral coil that
entwines all men, obscuring the clarity of vision that Schadau now attains.

In this radically altered state of consciousness Schadau is present at a most
enlightening scene between the goddess of the Seine, who has just risen from
its waves, "a half-naked female, illuminated by the moonlight," and "a
woman of stone, immediately next to me, who supported the parapet upon
which the three princely plotters had stood" (1:68). Complaining of the
procession of blood-drenched corpses staining her waters, the river goddess
expresses her annoyance in decidedly un-godlike language, "Pfui, Pfui!",
and asks her "sister" the reason for all the killing: "Are the beggars whom I
see washing their rags in my waters of an evening driving out the rich?"
(1:68). The caryatid whispers in response, "No . . . they are murdering each
other because they can't agree about the proper road to bliss," at which
point Schadau notes that "her cold countenance contorted itself into an
expression of scorn, as though she were laughing at monstrous stupidity"
(1:68).

Within the context of Schadau's OOBE it is impossible to know with
certainty whether the river goddess and the caryatid exist subjectively or
objectively. Meyer does not elaborate their mode of existence. They may be
archetypes from Schadau's unconscious, projected outward onto the embat-
tled city-scape, since the inner barriers between the conscious and unconscious mind are lifted with release from the body during an OOBE. On the
other hand, they may be veridical hallucinations, that is, objectively valid
astral beings that exist in a dimension outside the normal space-time con-
tinuum and can only be perceived from within that dimension.[17] It is also
well to bear in mind that the subject-object distinction is regarded by
mystics as an illusion of conventional consciousness, so that the whole
question of ontology may be inappropriate. In any case, their function
within the narrative remains the same, and it is a more complex function
than has generally been assumed. Critics have focused exclusively on the
caryatid's ironic remark, accompanied by mocking grimace, about the stupidity of religious fanaticism, identifying this as Schadau's profound insight
and/or Meyer's own point of view.[18] What they have failed to see is that
Schadau's perception is here clairvoyant and must be regarded in its entirety
as a *Gestalt*. To reduce it to a propositional statement about religious

fanaticism is to rob it of its vibrant symbolic resonances, both concretely visual and abstract intellectual. It is also to miss the function of the entire scene within the novella as a whole. It is essential to note that the river goddess and the caryatid, whatever their ontological status, manifest themselves to Schadau as intimately related entities. *Fluβgöttin* addresses *Steinfrau* as "sister." If we take this sibling form of address, in whatever sense the river goddess may intend it, as a clue to a dialectical relationship between the two, then Schadau's profound insight takes on a decidedly different cast from the usual interpretation of his moral transcendence of religious bias. In fact, we move out of the moral sphere altogether and into the metaphysical or cosmological. The river goddess is the spirit of changing social forms, of transitions from old to new orders. Her bloody stream is the violent flux of historical cataclysm. She is the upstart, the trouble-maker, and speaks appropriately in the street idiom of the revolutionary.[19] Her movement is as inevitable as the flowing of the Seine itself. The caryatid is the solid bulwark of cultural tradition. She is not, as Hertling says, the "Trägerin des Louvredaches,"[20] but the bearer of the parapet "upon which the three princely plotters had stood" (1 : 68), hence the "bedrock" ("Steinfrau") of the established order. Though opposites, these historical forces are nevertheless *Geschwister,* each eternally evolving out of the other in dialectical interdependence. Seen together, they embody allegorically not merely the struggle of the Huguenots, bound by particulars of time and place, to broaden the scope of the rigid Catholic establishment, but the very cosmology of historical movement itself. Meyer portrays a similar symbiotic relationship between change and tradition or movement and stasis in the famous lyric, "Der römische Brunnen."

It is not only in their visual aspect that the river goddess and the caryatid symbolize history as dialectical movement. The very form of their verbal exchange, the question and answer, is also dialectical on the level of logic or thought process. Meyer was certainly no Hegelian; his historian-mentors were, among others, Ranke (an outspoken opponent of Hegel), Burckhardt, and Michelet. Still, the dialectical principle, whether in the triadic form given it by Hegel or otherwise, was part and parcel of nineteenth-century intellectual life, and the notion of the extension of this principle from the realm of thought and language into nature and history was in Meyer's time an internationally popular one. It had its ancient origins in such thinkers as Heraclitus and Proclus and its nineteenth-century exponents, even apart from Hegel and the German romantics, in Coleridge, Emerson and the French philosopher, Victor Cousin.[21] Meyer, a voracious reader in French history and philosophy, may well have read Cousin's Hegelain *Introduction à l'histoire de la philosophie,* although there is no evidence that he did. In any case, he makes creative use of the dialectical idea by having the verbal exchange between *Fluβgöttin* and *Steinfrau* imply through its dialectical form an extension into the metaphysical process of history, which the two figures visually symbolize.

If, then, one views this scene as Schadau's attainment of metaphysical rather than moral insight, if his epiphany is the realization, not that fanaticism is evil, but that history will take its inevitable course, using human conflict as its vehicle of self-realization, then the caryatid's sarcastic response to her "sister's" question is a comment on the inability of most mortals in their shrouded consciousness to perceive the true pattern of history rather than a preachment against the moral deficiencies of human character: " 'They are murdering each other because they can't agree about the proper road to bliss.' And her cold countenance contorted itself into an expression of scorn, as though she were laughing at monstrous stupidity" (1:68). It is human ignorance that the caryatid mocks, not evil behavior; it is man's remoteness from the cosmic perspective, not his malevolence, that makes him an object of the laughter of the gods. The distinction between the metaphysical and the moral is crucial, because on it rests the entire matter of Meyer's thematic and formal intent in *Das Amulett*. Schadau's insight into the cosmic pattern of history, accessible only in a bodiless state of clairvoyance, is the most dramatic sequence in a novella whose inner compositional principle is the problem of discontinuous levels of historical consciousness. It is Meyer's artistic preoccupation with this problem of human consciousness, cast in its contemporary historistic mold, and not his moral interest in indicting human bigotry, that provides the key to *Das Amulett*.

The rich vein of irony inherent in Meyer's theme becomes apparent the instant Boccard enters the room, for it is at this point that Schadau loses the cosmic vision he had attained during his OOBE. Boccard's sudden entrance dispels the vision and forces Schadau's consciousness back into his body: "At this moment the door squeaked. I was startled out of my drowsiness and caught sight of Boccard" (1:68). Immediately it is evident that Schadau has lost the significance of this rare experience, since he implores Boccard for information regarding the violent events whose underlying meaning he has just penetrated more deeply than anyone else: " 'For God's sake, Boccard,' I cried and plunged toward him. 'What happened this past night? Tell me! . . . Is the blood bath over?' " (1:68). Re-entry into the body has resulted in a contraction of Schadau's consciousness from the dispassionate, Olympian perception of universals to an impassioned, self-interested concern for specific details, above all, concern for his wife: "Now the thought of Gasparde flashed through my brain like heat lighting; everything else disappeared in darkness" (1:68). The irony of this last clause is, of course, that the first-person narrator is telling us more than he knows: unlike the reader, he himself has no inkling of what "everything else" involves. Looking back on this episode from a temporal remove of forty years, Schadau, as Jackson says, "is as blind as he was at the time." Jackson errs, however, in concluding from this that "His creator Meyer has no love for him,"[22] that Meyer's chief concern is to portray a hero whose lifelong moral intransigence he can condemn. Schadau's "blindness," even forty years after the massacre at the time of narration, is less moral than metaphysical. The function of the initial frame chapter, in which he displays a singular lack of sympathy for the wretched condition of the old Catholic Boccard, is to show that his Calvinist partisanship is as much a shroud over his perception of historical movement in old age as it had been in youth. His momentary God's-eye view of history, having occurred on a bodiless plane of existence discontinuous with embodied consciousness, has had no broadening effect on his historical myopia.

In the frame chapter, one also sees how Schadau's retention of his narrow Calvinist outlook into old age has assuaged his guilt over the death of his Catholic friend, Boccard, who had helped him and Gasparde escape the massacre. Observing the old man's frugality, he remarks with a sneer, "He gathers and hoards in his old age, forgetful of the fact that his family line will end with him, that he will leave his possessions to laughing heirs" (1:33). Only a rigid Calvinist convinced of the hand of Providence in Boccard's death could regard the old man's pathetic situation with such disdain. On the ride home after concluding his business with old Boccard, Schadau is overwhelmed by a flood of memories: "The images of the past rose before me with the aromas of the springtime earth with such urgent force, in such a vivid way, in such sharp and penetrating outlines, that they caused me pain" (1:34). But it is not the need to confess and expiate guilt that induces Schadau to record past events "to ease my mind in this way" (1:34), since, as has been seen, his religion has provided him with a convenient rationalization for any guilt. Schadau's need for relief is really a need for bodily release, a need to recover and assimilate the lost vision of his OOBE, which has left an indelible imprint on his unconscious. The tragic irony of his narrative search is that it yields no result beyond the recalling of a "dream" that took place upon his lapse "into an indescribable condition between waking and napping" (1:68). His admission that his descriptive powers fail to do justice to this condition indicates his vague inkling that there is more to the phenomenon he is about to relate than his memory is able to get at. The visual and auditory components of the OOBE are recalled and related, but the immediacy of metaphysical truth and the entire paranormal significance of the event are irrevocably lost to a reminiscing narrative consciousness that remains shrouded by the body.[23]

The split between mind and body, consciousness and action, grasping the pattern of history and participating in that pattern—this is the thematic and formal principle of *Das Amulett*. It appears in stark dichotomous outline when one places Schadau's OOBE, his sole moment of enlightenment, next to any number of incidents occurring before and after it that portray his historical vision as severely myopic: his duel with Guiche and its profound political repercussions to which he is blind; his confident dismissal of his landlord's fear of bloody reprisals against the Huguenots in Paris: " 'Don't be afraid,' I calmed him. 'Such times are past, and the Edict of Peace guarantees for us all the free practice of our religion' " (1 :60); his Calvinist scruples, resurfacing only moments after his vision, about appealing to Boccard for help "in the name of the Mother of God of Einsiedeln!" (1 :69), an appeal he can only bring himself to make after all others have failed; or his bigoted coldness toward old Boccard's misery forty years later.

Implicitly *Das Amulett* poses the questions: Is there some goal-directed pattern informing the chaotic events of history, and, if so, under what conditions can men perceive this pattern? Meyer depicts an optimistic answer to the first question but a pessimistic one to the second. The dialectical relationship between the river goddess and the caryatid reveals history's telic pattern of movement, but Schadau's capacity to perceive this truth only in a condition in which he is impotent to act on it, that is, out of his body, dramatizes the tragic darkness of conventional human consciousness. After Hegel and Darwin, the problem of discerning general laws governing historical change was one no serious writer of historical fiction could avoid. Tolstoy, for whom Meyer often professed admiration,[24] wrestled with it in *War and Peace* (1869), which appeared at the time Meyer was resuming work on *Das Amulett*. In his paragon of historical novels, Tolstoy poses the problem of human historical consciousness in terms that could serve as the perfect thematic abstract for Meyer's novella. Grimly the "omniscient" narrator declares:

> Nowhere is the commandment not to taste of the fruit of knowledge so clearly written as in the course of history. Only unconscious activity bears fruit, and the individual who plays a part in historical events never understands their significance. If he attempts to understand them, he is struck with sterility.[25]

This is precisely what happens to Schadau during his night in the Louvre. Up to then he has been a blind participant in the pattern of historical events. In killing Guiche he had unwittingly triggered the outbreak of violence against the Huguenots. There he was an *actor* on the stage of history. But as disembodied witness to the cosmic dialogue, he is a *seer*, and in seeing, he is "struck with sterility," for his insight is conditional upon the loss of the only instrument through which historical actions can be realized—the body.

The tragic split between grasping and making history is epitomized in Schadau, but, to one degree or another, it is a shaping principle of the other characters as well. The wise scholar, Chatillon, whose sense of history has matured far beyond the partisan squabbling of Schadau and Boccard, is to that extent impotent to act. Historical actions in *Das Amulett* are impelled by narrow factionalism, by more or less unquestioning commitment to either religious cause. Chatillon is isolated by his capacity to achieve an overview of the conflict, to see it in its historical inevitability as a *Gestalt*. His broadened consciousness depletes his motivation to act on behalf of his Huguenot comrades. Despite a firm intellectual commitment to their cause, "still he keeps," as Brückner says, "a certain distance from things by nature."[26] His niece, Gasparde, recognizes and accepts his deep-rooted pacifism out of love, though she has no inkling of its source. It is Schadau, and not her uncle, to whom she turns for help against the insulting Guiche: "I don't like to tell my dear uncle anything about it. Given his excitable and somewhat timid nature, it would disquiet him without his being able to protect me" (1:52).

Chatillon's tragic death at the hands of the rioting Catholics is also at least partially a result of what Tolstoy means by the sterility of understanding. No one could have sensed the explosive situation in Paris more acutely than Chatillon. Yet he takes no steps to protect Gasparde and himself from danger. His ostensible reason for staying in the city is that he wants to renew a commitment to his fellow Huguenots that he has failed in the past to uphold by deeds. Even here, however, his words betray rather a doom-ridden resignation than a commitment to decisive action: "I did not support my coreligionists as I should have; in this last hour, however, I will not abandon them" (1:64). The perspicacious Montaigne senses something of this when he chides the old man good-naturedly: "Old boy, you're deceiving yourself when you think this is a way of dealing courageously. You're doing it out of sloth. You've become too lazy to leave your comfortable nest, even at the danger that the storm will sweep it away tomorrow" (1:64). But Chatillon is far from deceiving himself. To the contrary, the tragic irony implicit in his ominous words "in this last hour" is that his heightened awareness transcends even itself: he is aware that his own awareness has rendered him impotent to act, even in order to survive.

Other characters in the novella may also be seen as variations on the inverse proportion between historical consciousness and action. Montaigne and Schadau's uncle both resemble Chatillon in their libertarian social attitudes formed from a broad overview of historical currents. Also like Chatillon, their heightened consciousness keeps them aloof from the scene of action. Montaigne, a freethinker, is long gone from Paris by the time violence erupts, and Schadau's uncle spends his years in scholarly seclusion on the lake of Biel in Switzerland, well out of range of the religious cold war being waged in the cantons. Gasparde and Boccard bring up the opposite end of the consciousness-action spectrum. Though she has little interest in doctrinal matters, Gasparde is a devout Huguenot and shares responsibility with Schadau for the fateful action taken against the hated Catholic Guiche. In using Schadau as her instrument to avenge an insult magnified out of all proportion by her own religious prejudice, she becomes in turn an instrument of the process by which history manifests itself. Boccard is a superficial hotblood given little to conscious reflection. His actions are impulsive, motivated as they are by two unexamined, and at times even conflicting, biases—religion and nationalism. His resentment of Schadau's Calvinism is mitigated only by his loyalty to Schadau as a fellow Swiss. His aid to Schadau during the massacre is not a reaching-out to a human being in need but a concession made to a Swiss compatriot who, in desperation, finally patronizes his superstitious devotion to the Virgin of Einsiedeln. It is "isms" that automatically determine Boccard's attitudes and behavior. His is a darkened consciousness that reduces him to the status of a pawn in the conflict of historical forces. As such he is Chatillon's antipode.

One other character, or rather fictional presence, is vital to the theme of levels of consciousness and to the form of the novella. Between title and first chapter Meyer inserts himself as translator of Schadau's memoirs with the announcement: "Pages yellowed with age, documents from the beginning of the seventeenth century, lie before me. I am translating them into the language of our time" (1:33). Commentators have noted the function of this device as a means of enhancing the verisimilitude and quasi-historical authenticity of Schadau's chronicle.[27] Beyond this, however, the fictional translator serves as a transcendent consciousness, a disinterested point of view located in both a literal and a figurative sense over and above the work, which encompasses the limited visions of the characters and, together with them, forms a hierarchy of historical consciousness. This perspectivistic hierarchy constitutes the novella's inner form. One might visualize it metaphorically as a set of Chinese boxes of awareness ranging from the all-enclosing historical vision of the author-translator-(hence) reader through a median area of enlightenment provided by Chatillon, Montaigne, and Schadau's uncle down to the smallest, innermost boxes of myopic partisanship evidenced by Boccard and Gasparde. Schadau, as the central character who experiences a radical, though temporary, transformation of consciousness through his OOBE, moves from the innermost to the outermost box and back to the innermost. His momentary elevation to the God's-eye view of the translator imbues the inner form of the novella with a tragic dynamism, for his inevitable return to the body is a return to his role as blind instrument of the self-actualizing process of history.

Meyer's portrayal of historical consciousness over against action as a tragic polarity reflects the strong ambivalence he must have felt toward the prescriptive ideals of his "historian-father," Leopold von Ranke. Meyer read nearly everything Ranke wrote, and it is known from his letter of 4 May 1868 to his good friend, the Swiss historian Georg von Wyβ, that he had consulted Ranke's *Französische Geschichte, vornehmlich im sechzehnten und siebzehnten Jahrhundert* (1852–54) as a source for his depiction of the Saint Bartholomew's Day massacre in *Das Amulett*.[28] It is, however, less Ranke's historical studies than his historiographical principles that are relevant here. In *Über die Epochen der neueren Geschichte* (1854) Ranke poses a formidable challenge to the historian: "The deity—if I may venture to say—I conceive in this way, that it overlooks all of historical humanity in its entirety, being as it is beyond time, and finds it to be everywhere of equal value. . . . before God all generations of men appear with equal right, and the historian too must view the matter in this light."[29] Later, in a letter to King Max II of Bavaria (26 November 1859), Ranke speaks of the ideal that "would be realized if the subject [the observer of history] could make itself a pure organ of the object."[30] Intellectually, Meyer subscribed to this ideal state of historical consciousness in which all bias falls away as the historian becomes the pristine mirror ("organ") in which events are reflected. As Karl Fehr points out, it is precisely such an Olympian posture of "historical-pragmatic objectivity" that Meyer adopted from Ranke and claimed for himself as author of *Das Amulett*.[31] But Meyer's underlying ambivalence toward this ideal, particularly his doubting of man's capacity to perceive the pattern of contemporary history in which he is himself swept up and then to act with wisdom on that perception, is seen in the tension between intellectual assent and artistic intent in *Das Amulett*. While Meyer, as historical novelist temporally removed from his subject, can answer the Rankian challenge, his protagonist Schadau can only do so by relinquishing his sole instrument of historical action, his body. In an ironic sense, it is only as a bodiless consciousness that either author or protagonist can penetrate the metaphysical meaning of the conflict between Catholics and Huguenots. Obviously Meyer, for whom these events are past, can have no physical impact on them; his relationship to them is limited to the rarefied sphere of authorial consciousness. By the same token, Schadau, though a contemporary to the conflict, is no less impotent to act during his moment of illumination. And his actions after that moment has passed show no trace of that illumination. Both author and character are caught up in the mind-body split.

Even Meyer's intellectual assent to Ranke was not unwavering. Although able in his better moments to affirm a divine consciousness that both viewed and permeated history in its totality, he as often questioned his own, and by extension, man's capacity to rise above the constraints of ego and identify with its cosmic vision. Thus, in a letter to his cousin, Friedrich von Wyβ (27 July 1866), recalling the beauty of an Alpine landscape: "So I tell myself that the same Master who has ordered this has surely also drawn His lines, though they be for me hidden, in the totally different area of history, lines which guide and coordinate the whole."[32] This concept of immanent justice, a suprarational sense of the inherent rightness of events that Heinrich Henel has aptly called "a manifestation of mystic thinking in the realm of ethics,"[33] is the informing principle of Meyer's philosophy of history. It is just such immanent justice, the inexorable working-out of the mysterious hidden lines of historical evolution, that Schadau glimpses in the dialogue between river goddess and caryatid. The pity is that it is only for a flickering instant of transfigured consciousness that Schadau can, as Henel says of Meyer the lyricist, "surrender to powers (both without and within him) that are mightier than his reason and larger than his conscious self."[34] It was Meyer's ambivalence toward Ranke that generated the aesthetic impulse to *Das Amulett*, his attraction to Ranke's ideal of godlike historical consciousness, and his simultaneous skepticism of man's ability to grasp, and in grasping to shape, those historical currents, "larger than his conscious self," in which he is bodily embedded. The simple, unalterable fact of the physical grounding of consciousness in the present would forever prevent man, whether as historian, novelist, or otherwise, from fashioning for that present what Stendhal, with reference to the novel, called a "mirror of life," reflecting, as it "journeys down the highway," the "blue of the skies and the mire in the road below."[35]

In a larger sense, the ephemeral quality of Schadau's insight reflects Meyer's nostalgia, the nostalgia of a self-designated "child of the nineteenth century"[36] who felt himself an exile in his own time, for a bygone era before the all-embracing mystico-metaphysical world views began to be eclipsed by the piecemeal truths of an objective science. Although it is impossible to cite direct sources from this longed-for past for Meyer's portrayal of the out-of-the-body experience, or even to know whether he had any specific antecedent in mind, it is a fairly simple matter to identify various conceptions of the phenomenon from the recent and remote past which he doubtless came across in his lifelong study of history and literature. One could point to the Platonic view of the body as the temporary prison of the incorporeal, conscious component of man; or the out-of-the-body experiences reported by the great Swedish theosophist, Emanuel Swedenborg; or the allegory of Homunculus, the incandescent entelechy in quest of a body in *Faust II*. Meyer was well acquainted with these and other philosophical, mystical and artistic permutations of the mind-body mystery.[37] In his historical sketch of eighteenth-century Swiss town life written for the *Zürcher Taschenbuch* in 1881, "Kleinstadt und Dorf um die Mitte des vorigen Jahrhunderts," he relates an anecdote about an out-of-the-body experience involving the wife of a close friend of the young Lavater that had provided the inspiration for Lavater's first literary success, *Die Aussichten in die Ewigkeit* (1768–78).[38]

Even in his own experience Meyer the "realist" seems to have had at least a nodding acquaintance with mystical states of consciousness. During his recuperation from a nervous disorder in the pietistic asylum at Préfargier in 1852, he had employed some mystical technique or other as a means of establishing distance between himself and his illness. This momentary rising to a less ego-bound perspective on one's own oppressive situation, which is one way of describing what happens to Schadau, is mentioned in a letter to A. Meißner of 24 November 1877: "In those most difficult days [at Pré-fargier] I often got by with a modest bit of mysticism and found it—in mild doses—salutary, i.e., above and beyond subjection to necessity . . . I looked within my destiny, however it might turn out, for something to love."[39] Whether these "mild doses" of mysticism were self-administered during the hypnagogic moment between waking and sleeping, as is the case with Schadau, Meyer does not say, but it is known from Henel's searching study of the lyrics that this transitional phase of consciousness, this threshold to an awareness far superior to either waking or dreaming, had a special signifi-cance for Meyer the poet: "The dream states which Meyer describes [in the lyrics] are complicated by the fact . . . that both the subconscious and the conscious mind are active in them. They resemble the moment just before waking up, when reality intrudes upon the sleeper's visions, when he tries to 'get a grip on himself,' and when he is painfully aware of two worlds."[40] Schadau, of course, is not on the verge of waking up but, conversely, sinking into a kind of numbed hysteria, "into an indescribable condition between waking and napping" (1:68). Functionally, however, the two conditions are the same, each a potential point of entry into a sphere of awareness that lies above and beyond the normal waking-sleeping zone. All that is needed to reach this sphere is an impetus, which for Schadau assumes the form of a profound frustration of his need to escape that pushes him out of the waking-sleeping zone into a bodiless state of metaphysical illumination.

Perhaps the most intriguing speculation on possible prototypes for Schadau's OOBE is occasioned by the fact of Meyer's strong attraction to Saint Paul. Although Meyer never overcame his ambivalence toward the dogmatic aspect of Christianity, his admiration for the aggressive confidence with which Paul pursued his mission was unwavering. Through the spring and summer of 1860 in Lausanne, Meyer steeped himself in Paul's letters and in the Acts of the Apostles, intending to write a biographical sketch of the apostle.[41] The sketch was never realized, but the effects of Meyer's intense preoccupation with this charismatic personality were deep and durable. The influence of Pauline thought on *Das Amulett*, completed over a decade later, has been observed by Schimmelpfennig. It is an influence that extends even to the language that Meyer has issue from Schadau's mouth.[42] Whether Meyer resumed his study of Paul's letters during the writing of the novella or knew them well enough to paraphrase them in the novella from memory is not known. In either case, it is not unreasonable to suppose that Meyer was also familiar with Paul's concept of the psychic or spiritual body: "there are bodies that belong to earth and bodies that belong to heaven. . . . If there is such a thing as a natural body, there must be a spiritual body too" (1 Cor. 15:40, 44). And in following the exciting account of Paul's conversion in Acts 9, Meyer may well have had a lingering impression of an episode strongly resembling an OOBE related in the previous chapter in which we are told that Philip, after baptizing a eunuch, "was carried off by the spirit of the Lord, and the eunuch did not see him any longer; he went on his way rejoicing. As for Philip, he was next heard of at Azotus" (Acts 8:39–40).

In its historical setting and its implicit reference to various traditional configurations of the out-of-the-body experience, *Das Amulett* certainly reveals Meyer's strong intellectual and emotional ties to the past. Paradoxically, however, it is this very retrospective attitude that makes the novella a distinctly contemporary work of fiction. Through Schadau's out-of-the-body experience Meyer looks back wistfully to a time when it was still possible to conceive of the world and history as making metaphysical sense. But the futility of Schadau's moment of total historical consciousness, the immediate loss of that which is gratuitously attained, echoes a most contemporary nineteenth-century dwindling of faith in man's capacity to perceive himself as part of what Fritz Martini calls "a shared life-nexus of causes and conditions."[43] The fading of a transpersonal vision of life, of a world whose ordering principle emanates from a center beyond the narrow constructs of individual consciousness, lies at the core of German realism. Meyer's portraits of characters who stand at either end of the consciousness-action spectrum, characters who act without awareness or are aware but impotent to act, reflect his own and his era's increasing perception of human behavior as little more than a stimulus-response mechanism, and of historical awareness as having no impact on historical reality. In Schadau's out-of-the-body experience it is as if Meyer is lifting his hero up above the stifling miasma of his belief system by the scruff of the neck and demanding that he see, at least for once in his life, a transpersonal pattern of wisdom informing his own narrowly partisan actions. Through Schadau, Meyer objectifies and symbolically dramatizes his own crisis of metaphysical doubt. But the atmosphere in which the river goddess and caryatid reside is too heady for Schadau, and the author must soon allow him to be pulled down by the weight of an ego-bound consciousness rooted in the body.

The transitory character of Schadau's historical vision shows it to be an example of what Richard Brinkmann calls the "hypostasierte Ganzheiten" or reconstructed cosmologies from an earlier, more idealistic era that are built into many works of German realistic fiction. Thus do realistic authors take pains to elaborate the limited, perspectivistic nature of their characters' consciousnesses and proceed then to sew these tight pockets of awareness onto the comforting mantles of metaphysically ordered worlds, worlds that are, however, more products of nostalgic longing than confident conviction, worlds, as Brinkmann says, "which refuse any longer to be based on factual experience, but rather according to which particulars, experienced as isolated, are normatively arranged."[44] Schadau's out-of-the-body experience symbolizes the spiritual need of an author who has "trust in God, as much as a child of the nineteenth century can have,"[45] to get beyond a historistic world view that is merely hypostatized to one that is manifestly real. It is probably fortunate for us that Meyer never fully exorcized his own demons of doubt. If he had, the corpus of realistic fiction might well have been the poorer for it.[46]

2

Gustav Adolfs Page as a Tragedy of the Unconscious

IN the late 1870s, Meyer became drawn to the idea of writing a dramatic tragedy about the great Protestant standard-bearer of the Thirty Years War, King Gustavus Adolphus of Sweden. The king's loyal page, August Leubelfing, son of a Nürnberg patrician, was also to figure prominently in the action. However, as time passed a curious reversal of priorities began to occur in Meyer's imagination such that, by the fall of 1881, he was paying almost as much attention to the supporting character as to the protagonist. Thinking now about the royal page, and perhaps already glimpsing the rich narrative vis-à-vis the meager dramatic possibilities of his subject, he writes coyly to his literary mentor, Louise von François: "and Page Leubelfing, . . . yes, what becomes of him is my secret."[1] Of course, Meyer's "secret," revealed in the finished tale, *Gustav Adolfs Page*, was his intention to turn the historical Leubelfing into a girl, "Gustel," who dons the disguise of a male soldier, affects a stentorian baritone, takes her cousin's place in conscription and follows the king she idolizes to a glorious death in battle. The fact that the historical Gustavus Adolphus was known to have been severely nearsighted lent credibility to the improbable premise.

An astonishing footnote to this literary history is that Louise von François actually guessed Meyer's secret plans for a "sex-change operation" on Leubelfing, for in her response to his letter three weeks later, she facetiously envisioned the character of Leubelfing as "a Lutheran Joan of Arc."[2] But even more astonishing, perhaps, than this deft bit of mind-reading was her uncanny settling on none other than Joan of Arc as a point of comparison. In this, von François was positively prophetic, for if one translates the mythical context that, for example, Schiller creates for Joan in his dramatic prologue into psychological terms, it becomes clear that there is a far deeper bond betweeen these two heroines than the enchanting image of the militant maiden. Viewed psychologically, both suffer under the prohibition by the father against feminine experiencing. In *Die Jungfrau von Orleans* Schiller makes God the mythical equivalent of the dictatorial father who forbids his daughter the natural joys of sexual love and motherhood for the sake of a "higher" destiny he holds in store for her.[3] Meyer, on the other hand, penned *Gustav Adolfs Page* at a later time, when an author was as likely to draw inspiration from the philosophical and sociocritical antecedents of modern depth psychology as from mythological conceits in his portrayal of familial conflict. Coming under the sway of these nascent psychological ideas, he weaves his tragic narrative, as I will show, out of an unconscious tension in Gustel between her stifled natural feminity and the masculine persona foisted upon her by an insensitive father and ironically emblematized by her male page's disguise. A further irony is that the change of sex from male to female to which Meyer subjected the historical Leubelfing has its precise mirror-image in the theme of his story: the maiden's unconscious quest to become a man for her father. It is possible, though one cannot be certain, that the idea of the historical liberty sparked the narrative theme in Meyer's mind by reverse association.

The why's and wherefore's of Gustel's unconscious dilemma occupy our attention here, for it is only when read psychologically as a tragedy of the unconscious that the full aesthetic power of Meyer's story is released. Curiously, while some critics have alluded to the interplay of unconscious designs within and between the characters, no one has taken the subliminal dimension of the narrative seriously enough to trace its clear omnipotence over the life and death of the heroine.[4] This is especially puzzling with respect to the critical literature appearing since 1950, when evidence of the role played by *Gustav Adolfs Page* in Freud's formation of the early psychoanalytic concept of deferred action came to light.[5]

More generally, Freud's letters to Fliess reveal an intense preoccupation with Meyer's works during the few years preceding the publication of the historic *Traumdeutung* (1900), critical years for the working-out of such fundamental theories as the family romance and the Oedipus complex.[6] All indications are that, for Freud, Meyer belonged in the heady company of Dostoyevsky, Goethe, Shakespeare, and Sophocles, a pantheon of intuitive psychologists blessed with the genial capacity "to salvage the deepest insights from the maelstrom of their own feelings quite effortlessly, insights towards which the rest of us can only blaze a trail with agonizing uncertainties and tireless groping."[7] One is impressed by the scientist's homage to the poet's intuitive gift; but, as I have suggested, there was more to Meyer's awareness of the hidden motives of the human heart than intuition: confirming and crystallizing this intuition was an intellectual familiarity with certain current proto-Freudian conceptions of the unconscious with which he came into contact through books and acquaintances. My analysis of *Gustav Adolfs Page* as a tragedy of the unconscious will close with a sketch of the confluence of some of these ideas in Meyer's thought. Taken together, textual analysis and intellectual-historical sketch argue for the profound effects of the emerging depth psychology on Meyer's artistic vision. Indeed, one discovers in this oft-slighted tale[8] that the psychological definition of Meyer's characters could at times go far beyond the patented sculpturing of revealing gestures and articulate facial expressions, beyond the plastic qualities of the *Augenmensch* for which he is so well known, to the intricate creation of characters whose entire strategies for living are shaped by motives and conflicts parted from their own normal waking consciousness, as William James so aptly phrased it, "by the filmiest of screens."[9]

My thesis that the unconscious is the locus of all significant action in *Gustav Adolfs Page* rests on four cumulatively persuasive observations. The first of these—negative in character—is simply that, read straightforwardly as the tale of a young girl's patriotic hero-worship, this narrative, originally conceived in epic-heroic terms as "a drama of Schillerian proportions"[10] centering on the Swedish king, suffers from a misplaced focus of attention on a peripheral character, that reduces it to the trivial. This is, in fact, a criticism that has dogged the story from its earliest appearance down to the present day.[11] But it is inconceivable that Meyer's sure aesthetic instincts could have prompted him to abandon a momentous issue for a banal one, that there was nothing more at work in his turning from aristocratic drama to bourgeois novella than a self-indulgent impulse to fashion an amusing companion piece to Goethe's Klärchen. In his remark to Hans Blum linking the two characters,[12] it is clear that Meyer is alluding to Klärchen, not as a model for Gustel, but as a catalyst for the creation of a quite different character, whose "secret love"[13] for the king hints at needs and motives totally alien to the artless quality of Klärchen's love for Egmont. Something about Klärchen's heedless devotion must have suggested to Meyer a psychological possibility intriguing and weighty enough to allow him to drop the cherished idea for a dramatic tragedy of royalty without suffering the artist's grief over an "unborn child." I propose that the only sufficient cause for this would have been a "secret love" in Gustel conceived by the author as "unconscious love," a lifelong unacknowledged yearning for the father who never accepted her and, upon his death, for the king as a father-substitute. This yearning gathers up within its smoldering impotence all the important themes of her personal history and is played out on the always-curtained stage of the unconscious where each individual is his own highborn protagonist.

My second observation concerns the intense anxiety, at times escalating to panic, that plagues Gustel from the moment she arrives in the Swedish camp near Nürnberg in her male page's disguise. Ostensibly, she fears the puritanical king's harsh censure, should he see through her ruse ("Such moments [when the king seemed to sense something] caused the page a sudden fear" [2:41]), and the stain on his honor that exposure by a third party would bring. Reasonable grounds for apprehension, one might assume at first glance, and yet the relentless, almost savage quality of what can only be called her dread ("the page had become extremely worried to the point of distraction about her disguise and her sex" [2:44]) seems decidedly out of proportion to the issue. She has, after all, entered into this deception for the very noblest of motives, to serve and protect her king, if necessary even with her life; indeed, so bizarre a deception could only be viewed as an indication of the lengths to which she is prepared to go to express her devotion. Subjectively at least, Gustel would have every reason to feel at peace with her own motives. Moreover, late in the story she is assured by her godfather, Colonel Ake Tott, whom she meets in her hysterical flight from camp, that women disguised as soldiers are a common fact of camp life over which no one is raising any eyebrows, and that, in fact, "you weren't exactly risking your neck. If he'd found you out, he [Gustav Adolf] would have scolded you with 'Beat it, you foolish brat!', and a moment later he'd be thinking of something else" (2:57). All of this leads one strongly to suspect that the true and sufficient cause of Gustel's exaggerated fear of exposure is hidden even from herself and is at bottom the threat of self-exposure. It is the threat of intolerable insight into the true meaning of her feelings for the king that feeds her anxiety, a threat consciously symbolized and masked by the, at best, marginally legitimate concern over exposure to others.

Thirdly, one observes a curious ambiguity surrounding the chronology of Gustel's birth and her parents' marriage, background exposition conveyed to us in chapter 1 through repartee between Gustel and her relatives, old Uncle Leubelfing and his son, August. From the old man it is learned that Gustel's father, Rupert, a soldier in the Swedish service, had married her mother at seventeen and been killed in a brawl at thirty. Yet Gustel has previously mentioned that "until I was almost fifteen I was always on horseback with my mother and father and wore just my short riding outfit" (2:36). If one takes Gustel literally here, one cannot avoid the author's possible insinuation that young Rupert assumed the burdens of marriage and parenthood with some reluctance, perhaps yielding to pressure to provide his lover's expected child with a name. This line of speculation is supported by Gustel's enigmatic revelation that her father "fell in defense of my mother's honor" (2:37)—enigmatic, that is, until the reader, having just been alerted to the ambiguous circumstances of Gustel's birth, deduces from the remark that her father was killed attempting to avenge some loose-tongued cohort's slurring allusion to his wife's sexual indiscretion. Taken together, these veiled implications give one pause to question the true nature of the emotional bond between father and daughter.

Interestingly, Burkhard and Stevens, the only critics to have noticed the chronological anomaly, do not even entertain the interpretive implications of a "shotgun marriage" between Gustel's parents, preferring instead to censure Meyer for a "lapse" in "accurate attention to chronology."[14] I suggest, however, that Meyer was too much the "bleeder," the painstaking stylist and careful architect of plots, to have made so significant an error, notwithstanding his description of the genesis of *Page* as "a sudden idea that I carried out without interruption,"[15] and that the chronological ambiguity is a deftly planted clue to the unconscious forces that shape the adult behavior of this unwanted child. What emerges, then, as the dominant theme of Gustel's life is her desperate struggle to win the love of a reluctant father, an impetuous "roughneck" (2:36), as old Leubelfing sees him, who, hardly more than a boy himself, was not nearly ready for the moral and emotional responsibilities of parenthood that were suddenly thrust upon him.

Gustel's struggle to win her father's love ensnares her in a conflict between true and false identities, between the person nature intends her to be and the persona she believes she must become to please her father. This brings me to my fourth observation, which is of a key image that occurs quite subtly in the first chapter while recurring more conspicuously in the second. The image functions as the author's emblematic indication to the reader of the irony implicit in Gustel's unawareness of her identity conflict and of the specifically sexual form which the conflict assumes. In the opening scene Meyer has just introduced Gustel in terms more befitting a virile youth than a modest maiden: "A girl as supple as a poplar tree entered the room. She had laughing eyes, short hair, the figure of a boy, and rather cavalrylike manners" (2:35). After dinner, as she prepares to listen to the Leubelfings' tale of woe concerning August's impending conscription as a royal page, the author says that she "shoved back her chair, and folded her arms. She crossed her slender legs under her blue skirt with its pouch and keyring hanging from the belt" (2:36). The image of the juxtaposed pouch and keys suspended from her belt in the general vicinity of the pelvis would not of itself evoke associations to the male and female genitals, were it not unequivocally reinforced at the beginning of chapter 2 as the queen, in her fussy admonition to the new page not to shrink from the little sartorial tasks that go with the job, "put it [a silver thimble] on a finger [of the page]" (2:39). The king, who has been silently observing Gustel's disgusted reaction to this unexpected "woman-ish" side of soldiering, "now burst out in hearty laughter as he caught sight of his page with a short sword on his left hip and a thimble in his right hand" (2:39). The image of the keys and pouch in the earlier scene, mentioned only casually by the narrator in a subordinate clause, is here repeated as sword and thimble and is made the ostentatious focus of the reader's attention. The clash of genital emblems is no longer oblique but obvious. Gustel stands poised between them as if in mock-allegorical representation of the battle between the realms of light and darkness for dominion over her soul.

It also becomes clear from the context of the second scene that this configuration of conflicting genital images has less to do with physical sexuality per se than with the larger dimension of sexual identity. The reader's immediate association from sword and thimble to phallic and vaginal does not stop there but moves on to an awareness of a fundamental male-female antagonism within Gustel, a primal struggle between natural and artificial gender identities by which she is unconsciously gripped. One could say here that the ludicrous pairing of genital images underlines an internal conflict that is essentially sexual-political. It is, after all, the amusing way in which Gustel's *tableau vivant* unwittingly violates the code of "separate but equal" sexual *roles* (protector vs. protected, destroyer vs. mender), that tickles the king's funny bone, and not an association to the sexual organs that he would not be likely (consciously) to make. The reader also becomes aware at this point that Gustel's donning of the soldier's uniform, done with the conscious intention of merely *pretending* to become a man, represents an unconscious wish *truly* to become one. The male uniform superimposed on the female body symbolizes the suppression of the feminine principle by the masculine in Gustel.

"The entire complex of feelings and fantasies that have for their content the woman's feeling of being discriminated against, her envy of the male, her wish to be a man and to discard the female role, we call the *masculinity complex of woman*," Karen Horney writes in 1926 (italics hers) and alludes to Schiller's Joan as a literary prototype of the aberration.[16] She could as well have pointed to Meyer's Gustel and to the roots of the complex in Gustel's disturbed relationship with her father, a relationship that appears anything but disturbed until one looks closely at old Leubelfing's and her own casual reminiscences in chapter 1. The implication from these, mentioned above, of a marriage forced upon an adolescent father with many wild oats left to sow and not a thought of parenthood in his head, is the vital clue signaling us to look for trouble in Gustel's self-imagined childhood paradise. How does such a man-child deal with the terrifying trap of involuntary fatherhood? He deals with it by not dealing with it: by psychologically denying its reality. When Gustel mentions that she has never quite gotten used to skirts, that as a child she spent most of her time in riding breeches becoming an expert horseman in the company of her father, and when it is later learned from Ake Tott that Gustel rode with her father's regiment "until she was fourteen and more" (2:56), it becomes apparent that the father escaped the parental trap by turning his daughter into an army crony. To the extent that he was able to mold Gustel in the image of an apprentice comrade-in-arms, effectively making her into the only kind of person to whom he could easily relate—a member of his male regiment—to that extent he managed psychologically to deny the fact that he had a child. Moreover, in having been made by her father into a crony, Gustel was deprived not only of her status as a child, but of her femininity as well. Had Gustel been a son, the damage caused by the father's need to deny parenthood would still have been great; as it is, the damage is incalculable.

Of course, nothing of this twisted scenario is evident to any of the characters, least of all Gustel. On the surface and judged by Gustel's spirited assertions of pride in "my father's good name" (2:37), all had been sweetness and light between father and daughter. It is a measure of Meyer's skill as a psychological writer that he is able to convey the covertly destructive quality of the parent-child relationship without recourse to an omniscient narrator's psychic dissection such as we find, for example, in Keller's close tracing of Vrenchen's mental anguish in *Romeo und Julia auf dem Dorfe* or Mann's detailed anatomy of little Hanno Buddenbrook's creeping despair. The suffering of both children at the hands of brutalizing fathers is made palpable to us primarily through a discursive presentation by the narrator of their mental life. Meyer spins the tangled web of Gustel's emotions with hardly a lapse into such "non-artistic" explanatory modes of characterization. Nor does he allow an especially insightful character to speak for him in calling the reader's attention to Gustel's hidden plight (as he does, for instance, with the sagacious Fagon vis-à-vis Julien Boufflers in *Das Leiden eines Knaben*), since his artistic purpose is precisely to construct a world in which human beings act out of motives beyond their own or anyone else's immediate awareness or control. (The one possible exception to this—Ake Tott's observations in chapter 4—is discussed below.) Meyer limits himself to purely literary means in evoking the subtle sway of the unconscious: the use of ironic symbol, the gentle nudging of the reader towards inferences based on the characters' offhand remarks, and, most revealingly, the gradual establishment within the heroine of a pattern of behavioral and attitudinal details that points toward a dominant life-directing intention not evident from any single act or attitude by itself.

As we have seen, the chronic dread of exposure that grips Gustel in camp, out of proportion to any realistic threat of reprisal, is part of this pattern. So, too, the contempt she displays in the opening chapter for anything that reinforces her jaded conception of feminity as trivial, weak and pusillanimous. Thus her arrogant spurning of the company of the local women, with whom she had refused to sit during the king's reception, as "limp" and "silly"; her churlish aversion to the encumbrances of a woman's skirts: "women's dresses don't fit me"—pants provide the mobility she needs for the manly activities she prefers; her tongue-in-cheek suggestion to cousin

August, who fears conscription, to hide among the giggling girls, "just like young Achilles here in the fancy work on the stove tiles. And when crafty old Ulysses spreads out the weapons in front of them, don't you go leaping for a sword" (2:37).

Toward the end of this scene, as the disguised Gustel is about to leave with the cornet, she performs two acts in quick succession that clearly show how both her fear of exposure and contempt for femininity are inextricably linked to the dominant unconscious craving for her father's love and approval. Upon taking leave of cousin August, "switching suddenly to unconstrained gaity, the 'page' seized young Leubelfing's right hand, pumped it up and down, and cried, 'Farewell, sweet [female] cousin!' " (2:38). This mock-ceremonious exchange of identities is, in the fashion of most jokes, the conscious expression of a profoundly earnest unconscious aim: Gustel symbolically consigns her femininity to the male cousin who needs it. At the same time, in donning her father's uniform, she courts his approval by literally identifying with his rejection of her femininity. In fact, in its most elemental sense, the donning of the uniform becomes a ritual of *total* identification. By "becoming" her father, she attempts, if not to fill, at least with his sartorial effigy to cover over the inner void where his love should be. Rather than incorporating the love-object, she has herself incorporated *by* it, an expression of her passive need to *be* loved.

The farewells completed, Gustel suddenly bristles at the cornet's move to slip his arm into hers to escort her out. Stepping back and reaching for her sword, she shouts: "Friend, hands off! I don't like to be crowded!" (2:38). An inexplicably harsh reaction to a friendly gesture, until one sees it as the first eruption of that dread of exposure that later plagues Gustel in camp. Once committed to masculinity, she must avoid any and all contact with men that could compromise this strategy. Any overtures from men that could evoke even the slightest stirrings of feminine feeling and thus undermine the repression are from now on taboo. Any experiencing of herself as a woman can only alienate her father further. (The fact of her father's death is no deterrent to this aim of her unconscious, where the reality of death is mitigated by the illusion of introjection. The father lives on as a phantom of Gustel's inner world, his death only serving to intensify her strategy.) Both acts, then, the joking farewell to her new *Base* (female cousin) and the repelling of the cornet's gesture of contact, are part of Gustel's monolithic unconscious quest to win her father's love by becoming a man for him.

Gustel's overvaluation of things male and denigration of things female—her masculinity complex in Horney's sense—is not simply a matter of errant pride or eccentric preference, but of psychological survival. Her tragedy is that the conditions for her survival, not to speak of growth and fulfillment, are impossible and condemn her to an existential impasse between gender identities. Neither can she become a man, nor can she as a woman effect a *rapprochement* with her father in reality. His death ensures his survival in her unconscious as an implacable martinet.

Indeed, one may view the circumstances surrounding the father's death as aspects of an event of "critical mass" that irrevocably locks Gustel into her present impasse. As has been seen, the chronology establishes that he was violently struck down when Gustel was about thirteen, that is, near the onset of puberty when all the early unresolved issues of the Oedipus complex reassert themselves with great force. Horney argues that women who display obvious masculinity strivings have passed through a phase of unusually strong father fixation in early life, thus attempting, in the first instance, to resolve the Oedipus complex in the normal way by retaining their original identification with the mother and, like her, taking the father as love object. It is only when this strategy fails, that is, when her love is unrequited, that the daughter abandons the father as love object and shifts to an identification with him.[17] From this perspective, I interpret the death of Gustel's father as proof, in the logic of her unconscious, of the irredeemable failure of her efforts to win his love for herself as a woman and as cement to her conviction that she can only shine in his eyes by recreating herself in his male image. After all, if her womanhood had been acceptable to him, he would not have died. Moreover, if he was in fact killed "in defense of my mother's honor," becoming in the daughter's eyes a blood sacrifice on the altar of Demonic Womanhood, then the daughter would magically assume guilt for his death, to the extent that she had carried into puberty vestiges of that primal identification with the mother of which Horney speaks. She would actually have "learned" from his death that femininity kills and is therefore an evil to be despised and extinguished. She must therefore at all costs extinguish this evil in herself.

In this intricate shaping of Gustel's dilemma, Meyer illustrates beautifully the Byzantine ontological laws by which the unconscious operates. He shows it to be a world in which the protean exchange of identities, either in whole or in part, is routine, and in which life and death wear each other's hats in clownish collusion to dissolve the strict boundary that separates them in consciousness. In this world it is possible for Gustel to feel guilty for her father's death and to regard her own femininity as a murder weapon, while at the same time intensifying out of this very guilt her resolve to achieve the masculinity he has always demanded, as though he were now more alive than ever.

Entering the king's service under the identity of her cousin, Gustel is a veritable transference phenomenon waiting to happen. All the psychic liabilities of her relationship to her father now rivet themselves with demonic force to the Swedish monarch in whose close presence she commences to pass her days. She rides with him by day in his fruitless sallies against the Hapsburg foe, takes her meals with him by dusk, keeps his makeshift quarters comfortable for him, provides an ear for his complaints and a nodding head for his musing and moralizing. All in the shadow, eerily sensed by both, of imminent death in battle: "Leubelfing sensed it: the king was also on familiar terms with death" (2:44).

This sense of doom that envelops Gustel is enmeshed with an equally potent exhileration over the awareness that, at any moment, a stray bullet could end her impossible adventure. Indeed, in fantasy she challenges the bullet to strike her: "Then her eyes flashed as she joyously rode into a hail of deadly bullets, challenging them to end her uneasy dream" (2:44; the translation used here does not always adhere to Meyer's rule of referring to Gustel with the masculine pronoun, in keeping with her disguise). It is this perverse blend of scorching death-anxiety and an almost erotic daring of sudden death to take her that points to the transference phenomenon. With the reappearance of her father in the form of the king, Gustel has been given a second chance, as it were. By succeeding this time in becoming a man, a comrade-in-arms, she can "undo" the death inflicted on him by her own femininity. But it is at this point that the lethal paradox of Gustel's unconscious strategy traps her. The king is, in reality, not at all like her father. He is a thoughtful, sensitive man, generous with his affection:

> And afterwards, when the king roughed up her hair with a hearty laugh after catching her in some foolishness or at something she didn't know as he relaxed in the evening by the cozy lamplight, she would say to herself, all aquiver with rapturous happiness and fear, "This is the last time!"
> So time passed for her as death's proximity helped her enjoy the greatest moments of her life. (2:44)

Each time he reaches out to her in this way with fatherly affection, he arouses the buried yearning of a daughter ("herzliche Lust"), that most fundamental matrix of feminine feeling that can be repressed but never extinguished. In their surge toward consciousness these daughterly feelings evoke, so to speak, a double-tiered anxiety in Gustel. On the more profound level, they threaten to crumble the repression and confront her with the painful awareness of her unmet need for her father's love. At the same time, they generate, on the level of delusion or magical thought, a concomitant dread for the king's (father's) safety ("herzliche Angst"), lest her femininity kill again. And in unconscious anticipation of this "second murder," Gustel is flooded by feelings of guilt so intense that she all but commands the bullet to strike her down in retribution. Only in this light does the puzzling complex of feelings that grips her in camp make sense: her intense pleasure in the king's company, in apparent contradiction to her fear of his little intimacies, and her anxiety over their mutual imminent death, even as she invites this death for herself. The narrator obliquely confirms this view—but only obliquely, consistent with his eschewing of the omniscient explanatory mode—in summing up Gustel's days with the king as "transports of bliss,

. . . everything that only a youthful spirit can absorb and only a carefree heart enjoy before the moment of death from a bullet, or the moment on the brink of humiliating disclosure" (2:40). Through the equation of the "deadly bullet" with the "humiliating disclosure" via grammatical parallelism, the narrator is hinting that Gustel is prepared to accept death in atonement for any manifestation of her lethal femininity.

Meyer uses not only the grammatical voice of the narrator but the emotional reactions of the secondary characters as well in alerting us to Gustel's unconscious experience of the king as a father-imago, that is, an idealized version of the unloving father in reality. In the opening scene, cousin August lashes out at her in reaction to her arrogant scorn of his fear of conscription: " 'I have it!' cried the tormented boy. '*You* go to the king as his page! . . . Go on, go to your idol and worship him! After all,' he continued, 'who knows? Maybe you've had that in mind all along! Don't you dream of him anyway? You went all over the world with him when you were little [at her father's side], awake and asleep' " (2:37). Casting discretion to the winds of rage, August blurts out his private contempt for the obsessive mawkishness that has always characterized Gustel's attitude towards the king. To him she is a lovesick teenager who goes about in a chronic swoon over an airy idol. One notes here Meyer's subtle use of August as unwitting psychologist, who, in his offhand allusion to the inner, developmental structure of Gustel's obsession, says far more than he knows, but, in so doing, communicates to us exactly what Meyer wants us to know of the unconscious roots of that obsession: "who knows? Maybe you've had that in mind all along!" ("wer weiß, ob du das nicht schon lange in dir trägst?"). That August has struck a deeply sensitive nerve in Gustel is clear from her embarrassed reaction: "The girl turned away as a deep blush suffused her cheeks and forehead" (2:37).

This initial embarrassment in Gustel is paralleled near the end of the tale by a similar reaction that she registers to a related psychological thunderbolt, directed at her this time by Ake Tott. Having fled the king and the unbearable anxiety of that close relationship, she now sits in her godfather's tent at a remote outpost of the camp and listens to his recollection of an event from her early infancy. It seems the king had once taken baby Gustel from his arms and showered her with spontaneous affection:

"Well, I've always said, you shouldn't kiss little children. Kisses like that can sleep and then burst into flames when lips are fuller and more ready for them. You know, don't you, that the king took you out of my arms more than once? Cousin, he used to tickle you and kiss you with a great big smacking sound. You were a very lively and pretty baby." The page knew nothing of these kisses, and a deep blush was the only reply. (2:57)

If cousin August's outburst calls Gustel's embarrassed attention to the present-day manifestations of her obsession, Tott's recollection and "analytic" interpretation of the king's kiss give her an uneasy glimpse into its early origins. The obsession is grounded in the kiss of infancy that "sleeps" during the latency period only to "burst into flame" at puberty "when lips are fuller and more ready." Although Gustel cannot specifically recall the kiss, she does reexperience it somatically at this moment ("aber er empfand ihn wild errötend" [SW, 11:205]) and, in the extremity of her embarrassment, intuit the overwhelming power with which it has shaped her life. Literally, her fate has been "sealed with a kiss."

We thus learn from Tott that Gustel was indeed predisposed to make the king into a father-imago in place of the father found so wanting in reality. The astuteness of this seventeenth-century soldier's insight into psycho-dynamic processes borders on the anachronistic and probably reflects Meyer's eagerness to ensure that the reader pick up on the priority of the unconscious level of narrative action. Only here does he come close to indulging, through the mouth of a character, the natural urge of the narrator to explain.

These complementary episodes with cousin and godfather leave no doubt that Gustel's relationship to the king is to be read as an enactment of what Freud would later come to call the *Familienroman* or "family romance." (Indeed, as previously mentioned, Freud did cite Gustel's devotion to the king, in a letter to Fliess of 9 June 1898, as an example of "deferred action" motivated by the kiss in infancy. While *Gustav Adolfs Page* thus helped Freud to clarify his earliest speculations on the importance of childhood experiences in adulthood, the larger theory of the family romance was still in its germinal stages and would, in fact, draw heavily in its initial form on another story by Meyer, *Die Richterin*.)[18] In the family romance, the child, or in this instance, the fixated adolescent, seizes the opportunity to replace the unloving (read: deceased) parent in fantasy with an idealized version who ranks higher, or as here, highest, in the social order. The inference is clear from Tott's words that Gustel had already harbored such fantasies in early infancy and, from August's, that these fantasies had flared up again with enormous virulence during puberty with the traumatic event of her father's death.

In seizing on the king as a father-substitute, Gustel is attempting to use the deeply rooted fantasies of the family romance to provide a new ending to the Oedipal drama that had originally climaxed in what she imagines to be the father's fatal victimization by her own femininity. By becoming a male page ("man") for the king and eradicating every trace of a female sexuality she believes lethal, she hopes to undo the "primal parricide" and absolve herself of guilt. But the repression of one's very sexual matrix is too radical an act of self-alienation to be wholly successful, and one finds veiled expressions of the girl's need to give herself up to the "new father's" manly embrace subverting the ruse on all sides.

These veiled expressions occur mainly as fantasies whose sexual import is quite obvious to the reader but obscure to Gustel. In chapter 2, for example, the king peruses a book of maxims by various historical personages in search of a proper inscription of a signet ring he has in mind for his daughter. In keeping with fashion, the inscription should be some brief but telling expression of the wearer's attitude toward life. When Gustel, peering over the king's shoulder, points to the anonymous *Courte et bonne!* he takes her to task for her most un-Protestant "epicurean" taste. When he then asks her to specify how she thinks the expression is to be taken, she waxes ecstatic: "Solchergestalt, mein gnädiger Herr: Ich wünsche mir alle Strahlen meines Lebens in *ein* Flammenbündel und in den Raum *einer* Stunde vereinigt, daß statt einer blöden Dämmerung ein kurzes, aber blendend helles Licht von Glück entstünde, um dann zu löschen wie ein zuckender Blitz" (*SW*, 11:181). If she could, Gustel would condense all the energies normally dissipated over a lifetime into one hour of flaming passion ("*ein* Flammen-bündel") that would "give rise to a brief but blinding flash of happiness," dwindling down, in its turn, "like a quivering spark." The pyrotechnic metaphor is blatantly erotic and, in the expression given it by Gustel, closely parallels the lancet-arched rhythm of the sexual act. Indeed, Gustel envisions the ideal life in terms precisely befitting the climax of coition: "Courte et bonne!" Before the king can cut off this covert confession of desire during her pause for breath, she is again, in the narrator's words, "swept with passion" ("leidenschaftlich hingerissen") and cries out, "Yes, that's how I'd have it! *Courte et bonne!*" (2:42). Suddenly coming to her senses, she instinctively creates a smoke screen around what she has just come close to admitting by diverting attention to the multiplicity of interpretations admitted by the maxim: "Oh, Sire! Perhaps I don't understand it correctly. It has several meanings, just as the others do in your book here" (2:42).

Near the end of chapter 2, Gustel lulls herself to sleep with another, more delicate, but equally transparent sexual fantasy, this time explicitly involving the king. As she lies in her bed that is separated from his by only a thin partition, the reader is told that "It [her state of reverie] had all started from a silly childish realization that her name ended with the same syllable that his started with. Sleep put an end to her thoughts" (2:44). Gustel derives childish pleasure from the thought that their names are linked, in fact, literally fused together, by a common syllable: Au(gust)av. The fantasy of coupled names barely disguises the wish for sexual coupling.[19] One notes the narrator's care in pointing out that the fantasy arises at the threshold of sleep, in that moment of hypnagogic consciousness when psychological defenses are slack.[20] Also, his description of the fantasy as "a silly childish realization" cues us to its Oedipal roots.

Meyer may have an additional, symbolic intent in focusing the reader's attention on the common syllable, "gust," that fuses the two names. "Gust" or "güst" is an old agricultural adjective in the Southwest German dialect familiar to the Swiss Meyer and means "unfruitful," "infertile," or "milk-less." It is properly descriptive of mares and cows but, in the earthy metaphor of the farmer, may on occasion be applied to a woman. The other root syllable in Gustel's formal name (Auguste), "Au," means "meadow" or "pasture." When Gustel spins this fantasy of her link to the king by the common element "gust," she may be serving as Meyer's symbolic vehicle for telling us that, with respect to her womanhood, such a link can only be "unfruitful," that she is doomed to remain "a barren meadow" ("eine guste Au"), childless and sexually unfulfilled, as long as she persists in her unconscious game. A poignant irony emerges, then, from the contradiction between the unconscious erotic meaning of *gust* for Gustel with its procreative valence and this symbolic sense of barrenness as privately understood between author and reader.

This symbolism becomes more plausible when one considers it in connection with the event immediately preceding Gustel's fantasy in the same scene. Before drifting into reverie, she had been holding her ear to the partition to eavesdrop on the king, who was preparing for sleep. She could hear

> wie Gustav inbrünstig betete und seinen Gott bestürmte, ihn im Vollwerte hinwegzunehmen, wenn seine Stunde da sei, bevor er ein Unnötiger oder Unmöglicher werde. Zuerst quollen der Lauscherin die Tränen, dann erfüllte sie vom Wirbel zur Zehe eine selbstsüchtige Freude, ein verstohlener Jubel, ein Sieg, ein Triumph über die Ähnlichkeit ihres kleinen mit diesem großen Lose. (*SW*, 11 : 185)

Gustav prays, almost demands ("bestürmte"), that God take him in the fullness of manhood ("im Vollwerte"), before he should become, as he revealingly phrases it, "a superfluous or disabled man." In secret, Gustel first sheds tears of pity, but, in the dialectical rhythm of emotions, this surface reaction suddenly yields to a deep, selfish joy, a darkly powerful rush of triumph as she senses that their destinies are somehow tragically parallel. Clearly, Gustel's unconscious is momentarily attuned to that of the king. His manifest prayer for deliverance from a potentially disabling injury in battle expresses, even as it conceals, a profound fear of sexual impotence, resulting rather from the ravages of age and worry over war than of war itself. It is from *this* disability that he would be spared, one that would make him, in a way he could not endure, "a superfluous man." Far better to be taken "im Vollwerte." The sinister joy that wells up in Gustel, blotting out the conscious tearful pity, springs from her unconscious identification of the king's sexual anxiety with her own. It is the sad, desperate joy over having found a fellow sufferer, a joy she rationalizes to herself as a kind of devil-may-care attitude towards the physical dangers they face together in battle. This emotion then leads directly into the name-coupling reverie with her drowsy doting on the common *gust*. One sees, then, how the symbolic wordplay functions in the larger context of the scene as a subtle clue to a sexual impasse that king and page suffer in common and that constitutes their common primal destiny.

In matters of the unconscious, it is a short, inevitable step from common to mutual suffering. Buried needs seek each other out. In a story suffused from first word to last with psychological irony, the most elaborate irony of all revolves around this latent fear of impotence on the part of the king. It is a fear that implicates him in a kind of unconscious *folie à deux* with Gustel which entangles her all the more hopelessly in her dilemma. One finds that the king, in compensation for his doubts about his own virility, unwittingly colludes with her in her reenactment of the Oedipal drama by accepting the role she has assigned him—but with a twist: for, whereas she would have him play the misogynous father to her masculinity strivings, his own need is to play the father who reaffirms his virility by seducing the daughter. Of course, this "seduction" never gets beyond frequent pats on the cheek and caresses of hair; but, as we have seen, such affectionate gestures arouse those dormant feminine feelings she longs but dreads to express ("all aquiver with rapturous happiness and fear"), with their attendant guilt, and, in so doing, are enough to drive her to invoke the only release from that guilt of which she can be certain: "This is the last time!" she consoles herself. Death will see to that.

That the king is unconsciously responding to Gustel, not simply as a woman, but specifically in quasi-incestuous terms as a daughter to be seduced is subtly suggested by his reaction of profound dismay to the letter from his daughter's governess. The governess reports that his daughter's tutor in French, ostensibly a Swedish Protestant gentleman of upstanding character, has been exposed as a devious Jesuit who had been secretly proselytizing the girl. While his outrage is certainly justified, still the king's couching of the priest's treachery in curiously carnal terms ("seiner geheimen bösen Lust, das bildsame Gehirn meines Kindes mißhandelt zu haben" [SW, 11 : 183]) prompts the reader's suspicion that he "doth protest too much." For several evenings he paces his quarters, obsessively brooding over—in his own words—"this misfortune, this crime," over this (Jesuit) father's (religious) seduction of his daughter, even after acknowledging that the girl could not have suffered any serious harm: "[The governess] was to make as little fuss as possible with his daughter about the matter; to treat it as just another bit of childish behavior" (2:43). One observes here the workings of a psychological projection: the father by blood disowns his own deeply repressed incestuous fantasies toward his daughter by casting them onto the unscrupulous behavior of this spiritual father. Illicit proselytism, the cunning seduction of a young girl from her belief system, is sufficiently analogous to sexual seduction to make the priest a convenient scapegoat. With this incident Meyer cleverly intimates the psychological basis for the king's unconscious collusion with Gustel. In the absence of his real daughter, Gustel serves as a substitute for the seduction through which he hopes to rejuvenate his flagging potency.

So the king's fatherly affection towards Gustel, at first glance a selfless expression, takes on, after all, its own sinister aspect. It should be noted here that the unconscious collusion masked by this affection is not just a reconstruction of mine based on inferences drawn from the king's behavior, but is explicitly suggested by Meyer in a fascinating passage that has him (the king) virtually "free-associating" to the ulterior erotic basis of his relationship with her. The reader is told that, in that welcome hour of leisure before sleep when he could relax and unwind, he would often tell his page "harmlose Dinge, wie sie eben in seinem Gedächtnisse *obenauf lagen*" (*SW,* 11:179; my emphasis), that is, things told, literally, "off the top of his head" in apparently random sequence. Sometimes the sexual motive in these musings would be only obliquely expressed, as in his anecdote of the "pompous sermon . . . he had heard at the Court Church when he went to Berlin to get married" (2:41), in which, as Freud has observed with respect to dreams,[21] the insignificant image (the sermon) holds the spotlight while the revealing one (the wedding) is relegated to the background. At other times, however, the king's idle chatter would come within a hair's breadth of laying bare his tacit approval—indeed, eager abetting—of Gustel's unconscious designs, as in "the incredible story of how they had told *him,* the King!, after the birth of his child that it was a boy, and he had let himself be deceived for a while" (2:41). One can scarcely imagine a clearer signal to Gustel to continue her transvestite masquerade (thereby making her desired feminine presence permissible) than this "offhand" recollection of having fondly indulged the delusion, at his daughter's birth, that she was really a son, hence, a male heir. At still other times, the narrator continues, he would tell his page tales geared to the fancy rather of a girl than a youth, for instance, "about parties and costume balls," as if

> the hoodwinked king, without being aware of it, felt the effect of the deception his page was practicing; as if the king were unwittingly savoring beneath the façade of a good-natured youth the playful charms of an attentive woman. (2:41)

"Without being aware of it" the king senses the deception; "unwittingly" he savors the charms of the woman. This is the author-narrator's sole direct reference, not only to the king's unconscious collusion, but, by extension, to the primacy throughout *Gustav Adolfs Page* of the unconscious level of narrative action. As expected, Gustel is plunged into panic the instant she senses in turn that he is playing to her hidden sensuality: "Such moments caused the page a sudden fear" (2:41).

The king thus becomes a totally ambiguous father-figure for Gustel. On the one hand, he is made by her into the authoritarian father who esteems only maleness and prohibits the expression of any feminine impulse; on the other, he is disconcertingly perceived by her as the seductive father who subverts his own prohibition. This contradictory bind is reflected in a sequence of punishment dreams that afflict Gustel, the first one occurring, "appropriately,"[22] during the sleep that follows her hypnagogic name-coupling reverie:

> But the page's dreams were not good ones, for her conscience intruded upon them. Images of judgment rose before her dreaming eyes: first the king, with furious eye and damning gesture, driving away from his side the unmasked page; then the queen chasing her out with a broom and with coarse words of anger such as never passed the well-bred lady's lips during the day; indeed, words she probably didn't even know. (2:44)

The roles of the royal parents in this punishment dream dramatize the twofold burden of guilt by which Gustel is crushed. Not only is she banished by the mother for violating the "normal" Oedipal prohibition against a liaison with the father (the queen "sweeps" her out of the family circle with a barrage of uncharacteristic gutter language that aptly expresses the "debased" nature of her desires), but she is ostracized as well by the royal father's "furious eye and damning gesture" for the "sin" of feminine love. She is damned not only for loving but for loving as a woman.

While the king's role in this first dream is unequivocally that of authoritarian misogynist, a subsequent dream illustrates with brilliant succinctness the blurred effect that has crept into Gustel's image of him with the passage of time and the persistence of his subliminal overtures:

> One time the page dreamed her bay mare was running away with her. It galloped toward a chasm across a barren ground made red by an angry sunset. The king was chasing her, but before the eyes of her saviour or pursuer she plunged into the hideous depths to the sound of diabolical laughter. (2:44-45)

The configuration of conflicting forces that make up the relationship is captured in a handful of salient images and actions. Gustel is carried off by her runaway horse through a landscape (read: mindscape) described as "barren" (again, the barrenness theme) and "made red by an angry sunset" (the red condensing the misogynous father's anger and the mutual passion between her and the seductive father). Off in pursuit of her is the king, but the dreamer is uncertain whether his pursuit betokens the intent to stop the horse or spur it on ("saviour or pursuer"). The runaway horse embodies the repressed feminine desires over which Gustel is losing control. Will the king overtake the horse and help her regain control of it (that is, as misogynous father "save" her from being carried away by her "evil" feminine nature) or is his pursuit a sexual chase that is actually causing her to lose the reins of control? While the meaning of the bolting horse is clear, that of the king's pursuit remains pointedly ambiguous. The image of her plunge into the shattering abyss represents the dreamer's unconscious awareness of the psychic havoc being wrought by the paralyzing ambiguity of the relationship. But the resounding satanic laughter of the king that accompanies the plunge reveals her even deeper understanding that a clarification of his role either way would, in the end, resolve nothing. His laughter is a condensed image conveying the message that each of them has, out of his own motives, contributed to Gustel's unconscious transformation of the king into a two-faced demon, *both* of whose faces are lethal: no matter whether as the misogynous father she would have him be or the seductive father he would be himself, he is instrumental in her "fall."

The dream action strikingly anticipates the image of the bolting horse that seizes control from the rider that Freud uses in the *New Introductory Lectures on Psychoanalysis* to describe the ego's abdication to the id, or, as he puts it, "the not precisely ideal situation of the rider being obliged to guide the horse along the path by which it itself wants to go."[23] But Meyer's image has its literary ancestors as well. In Tieck's Romantic fairy tale, *Der blonde Eckbert*, the hero's dawning awareness of his incestuous relationship with his sister occurs on an aimless journey during which he allows his horse to go its own way.[24] And even predating the Romantics with their intense cultivation of psychic processes is the famous chariot metaphor spoken by Goethe's Egmont in which the id-tendencies are mythically projected as "invisible spirits" whose relentless whiplash drives "time's solar horses with our destiny's fragile coach; and for us there remains nothing but to take heart and firmly hold the reins, steering the wheels out of harm's way, now right, now left, from a rock here and a drop there."[25]

Gustel's bolting-horse dream marks the dramatic culmination of the first two chapters, which make up, respectively, the exposition and development sections of the unconscious narrative. Since the unconscious scenario set up in these chapters is so elusive to a casual reading, elaborated as it is with studied subtlety, it demands the bulk of the interpretive work. Once this work is done, however, the final three chapters, ending with the deaths of king and page, easily yield their significance as a kind of "falling action," a series of tragically inevitable consequences decreed by the fatal blindness of each to his own (and their mutual) psychological reality.

Enter at this point the Duke of Lauenburg, a German *Reichsfürst* under the Swedish banner, and General von Wallenstein, leader of the Catholic opposition. Each, in his own way, quickly becomes a pawn in the unconscious, self-victimizing game being played by king and page. The first thing to be observed about Lauenburg is that he poses a real, imminent threat to the king's life. He holds Gustav responsible for the death of his concubine, the fiery Slav Korinna, who had taken her own life at the prospect of being sent by Gustav to a Protestant house of correction in Sweden. Moreover, adding insult to injury, Gustav has just humiliated him in the presence of the other German nobles for leading them in a pillaging raid on a group of defenseless refugees. So the unscrupulous Lauenburg is now hell-bent on employing all his savage cunning to gain revenge.

His significance, however, resides far less in the objective danger he poses than in the distorted unconscious interpretations that king and page place on this danger, which render them helpless to thwart his evil machinations. Gustel's first reaction to Lauenburg is one of shock over the resemblance of his voice to her own feigned baritone. As she listens from behind a curtain to his sarcastic rejoinder to the king's tirade, the reader is told that "at Lauenburg's first words, the page had flinched at the uncanny similarity between this voice and his [her] own. The same sound, the same pitch and timbre" (2:51). Once the king leaves the room, Lauenburg is free to spew out his bilious invective to the captive audience of princes, and the cutting edge of his hate-ridden voice sends waves of horror through Gustel: "Now his [Gustel's] fright became horror . . . [as] Lauenburg forced a laugh and exclaimed sharply, 'He curses like a stable boy, our Swedish farmer! By damn, we got under his skin today! *Pereat Gustavus!* Long live German liberty!' " (2:51). But the princes have been sobered by the king's anger, and they spurn Lauenburg's overtures of comradery ostensibly based on "German solidarity." As they make their exit one by one, Lauenburg sees himself subjected to the further indignity of ostracism by his peers:

> His expression became a grimace. In his rage the marked man balled his fist, raised it, and threatened either his destiny or the king.
> The page could not understand the muttered words, but the expression on the aristocratic features was so diabolic that the eavesdropper felt very faint. (2:51)

Meyer carefully implies that Gustel's horror is much more than an objective reaction to the implications of Lauenburg's menacing gesture towards the king. For one thing, the reader is told that she could not be sure at that moment just what the object of his seething anger was ("his destiny or the king"), since his muttering was beyond earshot. Then too, she is clearly shown in that instant as transfixed to the point of fainting by Lauenburg's satanic expression, hence beyond any capability of rational deduction. When one traces this spellbound horror back to its origins—her initial shock over the similarity of their voices—it becomes evident that the unconscious scenario is at work here. The extremity of Gustel's reaction to what is, at worst, an annoying coincidence of nature indicates that she is not seeing

Lauenburg for what he is, but is transforming him into something else—in truth, into an effigy of her own disavowed feminine nature, or, as she herself recognizes in a later, lucid moment, her "Doppelgänger" (*SW,* 11 : 202). Her appalled perception of their similar voices is a manifestation in consciousness of a perverse unconscious identification with Lauenburg as a lethal threat to the king. An accident of nature becomes the occasion for an intense flaring-up of Gustel's repressed anxieties about her own "lethal" femininity, a femininity that once killed the father and, now reactivated by this demonic doubleganger with matching voice, threatens to do so again. Thus "the expression on the aristocratic features was so diabolic that the eavesdropper felt very faint." That she "sculpts" her feminine doubleganger out of a *man* is explained by the congruence between Lauenburg as a deceitful male and her own deceitful male's façade. It is precisely the image of Lauenburg as the male who is not what he seems, the male who conceals a threat, that engages the symbolizing power of her unconscious to produce the identification.[26]

In the midst of all this, one notices how Meyer uses a feature of the interior decor to give palpable symbolic shape to these impalpable psychic events. The thick damask curtain that fronts Gustel provides an unobtrusive but unmistakable image for the inner barrier of repression by which she shields herself from full awareness of this crucial act in the unconscious drama. No more than the voice of the doubleganger is able to penetrate the "censuring curtain."

Gustel's re-creation of Lauenburg as the masked feminine self she abhors blinds her to his obvious intention to revenge himself on the king. Since she unconsciously perceives his threat as coming from herself, in effect, as an extension of the very power of her woman's nature to destroy that she has had to keep in check all along, she takes no steps to warn Gustav of the real danger that stalks him. Her gross distortion of reality leaves him exposed to his true enemy's treachery and results, ultimately, in both their tragic deaths.

It remains for Wallenstein inadvertently to set the wheels of psychic destiny in motion. This he does through his visit to Gustav late that same evening to warn him of a possible assassination attempt by one of his own men. Having overheard the suspicious dream-ramblings of the disguised Lauenburg, who had dozed off in his anteroom that noon while waiting to keep a business appointment, the general felt compelled by honor to alert his esteemed opponent.

Wallenstein's warning has momentous unintended effects, not only on the king but also on the page, who eavesdrops on the conversation through a crack in her bedroom wall. Meyer knew the unconscious mind to be the fertile soil of conscious superstition, and he ingeniously uses the image of Wallenstein popularized by Schiller—that of the great strategist obsessed by the occult causes of events, who cannot make a move without first consulting his astrological charts—to ignite in the heroine's unconscious the fateful explosion of magical thinking primed by the doubleganger experience. He virtually announces this intention in the narrator's remark prefacing the Wallenstein interview that "A vague feeling caused him [the page] to associate this visit [from Wallenstein] with his own fate" (2:52). While waiting for the king to appear, Wallenstein had been struck by the resemblance of the page's voice to that of the masked dreamer and had succeeded through a clever ruse in demonstrating a perfect fit between the glove left behind by the suspect and the page's hand. When he connects these clues to Gustel during the interview, the king scoffs: "I am ready to rest my slumbering head in my Leubelfing's lap" (2:54). But the king's assurances cannot pierce the armor of superstition that envelops Wallenstein; even if Gustel is not involved, he suggests, "I still would want no page around me, not even my favorite, whose voice sounds like the voice of the man who hates me and whose hand is the same size as my potential assassin's. That's going too far; it's tempting fate. That could be the end" (2:54). Of course, this irrational condemnation by resemblance plays right into the dynamics of Gustel's identification with Lauenburg. The entire overheard conversation was "like a ghost which made his [Gustel's] hair stand on end (2:55). She is incapable of making the obvious association of the clues to Lauenburg because she has unconsciously erased all distinctions between herself and him and is now overwhelmed by the conscious conviction that Wallenstein is, in some dark, unfathomable sense, right about her:

> Then the eavesdropper left his [her] post and staggered out into his room. Collapsing next to his cot, he begged heaven to protect his hero. Leubelfing's very presence—Wallenstein had said it, and now even the page was beginning to believe it—seemed to offer a mysterious threat to the king.
>
> "No matter what it takes," the page vowed in despair, "I'll tear myself away from him; I'll free him and make it impossible for my evil presence to harm him in any way." (2:55)

For his part, the king is also profoundly affected by Wallenstein's superstitious apprehensions about Gustel, despite his better judgment of their absurdity. When Wallenstein admits that the motives for his warning are not entirely noble, inasmuch as for him their destinies as opposed standard-bearers are interdependent in the same way that night and day can only exist in relation to each other, Gustav is suddenly vexed by the morbid thought that the general has been vouchsafed some astrological revelation of their mutual deaths: "Again the king thought for a moment. It was hard to suppress the assumption that some conjunction in the heavens or a configuration of the planets had shown the duke a common hour of death, one of them following the other with furtive steps and shrouded head. Oddly enough, this feeling suddenly gained authority over him despite his trust in God" (2:54). This reaction parallels Gustel's in its psychodynamic form: the abrupt clouding of the king's Christian belief by an astrological image alien to it, a momentary obliteration of his normal set of mind pointedly described, in the German, as "involuntary" and "forceful," indicates the surge to consciousness, in disguised form, of an unconscious idea: "Now the Christian king felt the atmosphere of superstition that surrounded Wallenstein beginning to infect him" (2:54). What has happened is that the king has come under veiled attack from his own conscience for his quasi-incestuous impulses towards Gustel. A harsh superego, steeled by the piercing Nordic winds of Stockholm and by its role as Defender of a loftily ascetic Prostestantism, has seized the cautioning Wallenstein as a projection screen from which to denounce those nightly flirtatious interludes with the daughter substitute. Since the king, in his self-appointed status as moral exemplar, could never tolerate even the faintest awareness of the drama of seduction, the internal accuser cannot confront him directly in its primary Protestant form but must itself go underground in order to come at him from an oblique angle. This it does by entering his awareness camouflaged as a disquieting sense of having been somehow infected by Wallenstein's superstitious fears regarding Gustel and, as he imagines, his astrological vision of their intertwined deaths.

Thus the uncanny sense of a link between Gustel and his own imminent death presses itself on the king's awareness. He "knows" it is only a temporary succumbing to the morbid idiosyncrasy of his visitor, but still the unwanted thought clings to him. He does not know the unconscious source of the thought's power. Wallenstein's warning, against all logic, that Gustel may be mortally dangerous to him is a projected warning from his own conscience against playing with sexual fire. The illicit erotic relationship with the daughter substitute, entered into to allay fears of impotence, must be renounced; it can only lead to psychological and spiritual death.

In the brief scene that follows Wallenstein's departure, king and page come to an ironic parting of the ways. The scene is a triumph of the awesome ability of the unconscious to ravage true communication by simulating it. Each senses the necessity for Gustel to leave, and each senses that the other senses this. But their unconscious motives for this tacit agreement, although congruent, are totally unrelated: Gustel perceives herself as a dire threat to the king's life; so too he. Moreover, each believes Gustel's covert femininity to be the source of the threat. But, whereas for her the danger of her sex resides in its proven potential for parricide, for him that danger consists in its power to lure him into the forbidden orbit of incest. Thus, under the hidden sway of the incest taboo, which he imagines to be an unaccountable "contagion" of Wallenstein's superstition, the king finds himself behaving as though Gustel were in fact suspect. Feigning nonchalance, "He playfully took the page's left hand and drew the soft leather over his fingers" (2:55). Contrary to all reason, he feels compelled to assemble evidence against Gustel as his would-be assassin. When she realizes he is doing precisely this, she is overcome by the ultimate horror of exposure: unconsciously she perceives the father to whom she would prove her masculinity as having seen through the façade to her noxious feminine core and interprets the glove's perfect fit as the final "proof" of that noxious core to both of them. His pronouncement, "It fits," carrying the weight of a condemnation by its stark simplicity, she reads as her cue to flee:

> . . . the page threw himself down before the king, seized both his hands and covered them with tears. "Farewell," he sobbed, "My lord, my everything! May God and all His Host protect you!"
> Quickly jumping up, he dashed from the room like a man possessed. Gustav rose and called him back. But the king could already hear the hoofbeats of a galloping horse. (2:55)

What was actually the self-condemning finger of the king's conscience, she has taken to be leveled at herself.

The king's attempt to call Gustel back is merely perfunctory. In truth, her departure is a relief to him, since it will enable him to carry out his unconscious resolve to renounce the seduction. The narrator is certainly alluding to this when he puts tongue in cheek and observes in a tone of mock curiosity that "—seltsam—der König ließ weder in der Nacht noch am folgenden Tage Nachforschungen über die Flucht und das Verbleiben seines Pagen anstellen" (SW, 11:202). The emphatic setting-off of "seltsam" by dashes points the reader towards this concealed motive for the king's failure to have his page retrieved. The strategic punctuation is then immediately reinforced by the narrator's offhand suggestion of an obviously false motive: "Of course his hands were already full, for he had decided to give up his camp at Nürnberg" (2:55).[27] Meyer has skillfully placed the narrator's affectation of ignorance in the service of the reader's illumination.

In flight from her waking nightmare Gustel gives free rein to "the horse's headlong gallop" (2:55). This image of the horse that, although galloping at full speed, remains under the rider's control counterbalances that of the bolting horse in Gustel's dream. There the horse, symbolizing the woman's desire, has usurped control from the rider; her passion runs away with her, as it were. Here we observe the contrary: the rider retains (passive) control by consenting to the animal's unrestrained run, each stride echoing her desperate desire to protect the father from herself by putting distance between them.

The horse as an objective image of its rider's emotions is then carried a step further in the rhetorical parallel drawn between the animal's gradual wearying and Gustel's calming down: "Gradually it [the horse] tired by itself at the camp's outermost perimeter. The rider's excited emotions also calmed down" (2:55). With physical distance comes a measure of inner clarity, the glint of a fresh perspective. The dizzying push-and-pull of strange emotions that has plagued Gustel for weeks finally resolves into an ever sharpening focus on Lauenburg as a doubleganger of her own making:

> More sober reflection . . . enabled the page to identify his double. . . . It had to be Lauenburg. Hadn't the page seen the marked man clench his fist and challenge the king's justice? And didn't the object of the king's wrath have a voice that sounded like his own? Wasn't he himself woman enough to have spotted in that one terrifying moment how small the prince's balled fist was? There could be no doubt about it; Lauenburg was planning revenge, was planning to murder the page's beloved idol! (2:55–56)

Through a rare use of *erlebte Rede* Meyer shows the first dawning of insight within Gustel. Although having no notion of how or why, she sees clearly that she has been viewing Lauenburg as a reflection of some unacknowledged aspect of herself and that this reflection has eclipsed the objective reality of his imminent threat to the king. She is oppressed by the irony that her flight, undertaken to ensure the king's safety, has only served to jeopardize that safety even further: "And this moment when the king was being pursued with uncanny stealth was the time he had chosen to banish himself from the threatened man's side" (2:56).

Strangely, however, Gustel's insight does not lead to effective action, for instead of dashing back to the king posthaste to warn him of danger, she can only decide "not to leave the camp. . . . 'I can fall in with some regiment and no one will spot me with all the marching and the fatigue. And then the battle!'" (2:56). For the present she will remain on the periphery of the encampment, neither too near nor too far from the inner circle. This settling on a middle ground, in effect a compromise between leaving and staying, reflects the fragile, tentative quality of her insight, for the compromise is at bottom one between reality and delusion. Although she now sees Lauenburg for the evil he is, she still cannot shake the feeling that that same evil also dwells within herself. To leave would be to abandon the king to the external enemy; to stay would be to expose him to the inner. The separation of identities must remain incomplete as long as the forces of delusion and fantasy remain themselves essentially intact, still lurking beneath the surface of her awareness, twisting that awareness to their own designs.

The most intimate of these fantasies belong to the woman, the "enemy within" whose exposure has driven Gustel away from the king. Relaxing her inner vigilance in the safety of distance and feeling the pain of sudden separation, she fills the leisurely autumn weeks at Ake Tott's station with erotic daydreams of the idealized father. Memories, gilded by yearning, drift through her mind of the days when she could enjoy his occasional touch and the nights when she could almost imagine there was no partition separating their beds: "Gustav Adolf was all the page could see in his mind's eye, even if in transfigured and unapproachable form. The days were past when the king would run his hand through the page's hair. Now the page no longer had his master beside him at night, separated only by the thin wall, and audible when he turned over or cleared his throat" (2:58). On one occasion, when she is detained in Naumburg on an errand long enough to witness the king's triumphal procession through the town square, she is brought to tears by a rush of love and hero-worship. But just as suddenly these emotions reveal their shadow side of intense jealousy as she sees the father gesture affectionately to her rival in the royal Oedipal triangle: "Tears welled from the page's eyes. But when he caught sight of the queen watching from a window across the square and saw the king wave a tender farewell to her, burning jealousy filled his heart" (2:58).

It takes an unequivocally sinister omen to jolt Gustel out of the clouds of fantasy back to reality. One day during maneuvers near Lützen, she notices the persistent circling of a bird of prey over the royal coach and is shocked by the image into renewed apprehension of the stalking Lauenburg. Unable to stay away any longer, she hastens back to the king, slipping into his quarters early the following morning during the bustle of preparations for the major offensive planned for that day. But even at this point not one word of warning issues from her lips. Indeed, one is struck by the fact that Gustel does not speak at all throughout this climactic scene. She is rendered mute by the fear that any utterance against Lauenburg will somehow magically turn straight against herself. Caught in a paralyzing nether zone between approach and avoidance, she is reduced to hovering nervously and unobtrusively at arm's length from the beloved father she would protect: "Now he [Gustel] made himself small in a corner, concealed by the officers' comings and goings" (2:59).

In the king, however, she finds an oddly transformed man who gives the distinct impression of needing nothing, least of all protection: "The king had finally finished issuing his orders. His mood was a peculiar one. . . . Did he already sense the truth and the mercy of the realm he felt himself so near to?" (2:59). Turning to the assembled German princes, "He gestured and spoke very softly, almost as though he were dreaming, more with his ghostlike eyes than through his scarcely moving lips" (2:59). Casting himself as a perceptive observer, the narrator suggests the basis for the king's unnatural serenity on the verge of a crucial battle: he has renounced the things of this world and resigned himself to death. Lützen, he is convinced, will number him among its casualties.

This otherwordly fatalism that has engulfed the king during Gustel's absence must be viewed in the light of his nettled reaction to Wallenstein's warning against her. What began as a seemingly trivial irritation over the general's ludicrous superstition has burgeoned into an irreversible poisoning of the spirit. Such a profound lapse into morbidity can only be accounted for in terms of the unconscious scenario. On this level, the warning was seen to be a projected sting of the king's own conscience, provoked by his seductive overtures towards Gustel as a substitute for his daughter. However, once forced by conscience to renounce the seduction, he is left with those haunting fears of dwindling virility that originally prompted it, and no permissible strategy for counteracting them. The renunciation of Gustel also implies that of the nubile daughter for whom she stands, since the unconscious does not distinguish between real and symbolic love-objects. In blanket fashion the incest taboo prohibits his use of the daughter or any image of her to bolster his sexual confidence.

On the unconscious level, then, I interpret Gustav's resignation to death as a final surrender to the fear of impotence. He announces this surrender in the opening of his last address to the German princes, consciously casting it in terms of a presentiment of disaster in the impending battle: "Gentlemen, friends, I feel that my hour has come" (2:59). One is reminded of that first masked expression of sexual anxiety, voiced in his distraught prayer to be taken "im Vollwerte . . ., wenn seine Stunde da sei, bevor er ein Unnötiger oder Unmöglicher werde." There it was seen how the apparent worry over a disabling injury in battle concealed a dread of the gradual crippling of sexual capacity (his "Vollwert") by wartime pressures. Here the king is shown as having capitulated to that dread; bereft by conscience of his means of combatting it, he has chosen to die rather than subject himself to it any longer. What began as a prayer, a wish, has now become a choice. This most private and intimate of defeats, by virtue of his very unawareness of having suffered it, lends strong pathos to the address which he believes to be his final public "testament": "Gentlemen, friends, I feel that my hour has come. I wish to leave with you my final testament. Not in matters concerning the war—those who go on living will take care of that. But, after my own salvation, in the matter of what you think of me" (2:59).

As he goes on to review the long, epic struggle to secure "the undefiled Word" of Protestantism in Germany, he is moved to reveal an ulterior motive for that struggle:

> "After the victory at Breitenfeld I could have dictated an acceptable peace to the Emperor. And with the Word secure, I could have returned with my booty like some bird of prey to my Swedish cliffs.
> "But I was thinking about German affairs. Not entirely without a desire for your crown, gentlemen! But truly, my concern for the Empire won out over my personal ambition. It must not belong to a Hapsburg any longer because it is now a Protestant empire." (2:59)

Almost by his own admission, the king's altruistic concern for the integrity of the Protestant religion in Germany is a rationalization of a secret "Gelüst" ("desire") for the German crown. In terms of the present discussion, however, the craving for political hegemony in that country must itself be seen as, at best, a partially successful compensation for the diminution of sexual potency. One must assume that the king's initial strategy had been to recoup the loss of sexual through the acquisition of political power. If he could no longer take a woman, he could at least take a country. In the end, however, this shift of interest from the primal sexual to the symbolic political sphere must have been half-hearted, otherwise his incestuous attraction to the maturing daughter and, in her absence, the daughter substitute would not have arisen. Having now been forced by conscience to renounce a girl already once removed from the truly coveted love-object, the king finds he can no longer sustain the much more remote displacement to the sphere of political conquest. If his renunciation of Gustel is a capitulation to conscience, his renunciation in his address of all political ambitions in Germany is a resignation to the complete failure of political power to compensate symbolically for the loss of sexual power: "Yet you are thinking and saying, let's not have a foreign king ruling us! And you are right. For so it is written: a foreigner shall not succeed to the throne" (2:59). The king's last address, delivered in the solemn tones of a Baroque ascetic who has cast off all ties to this den of *vanitas* and humbly awaits entry into the *Jenseits*, is, finally, the testament of a man who has been undone by a most nineteenth-century version of unconscious determinism.

The scene climaxes in a powerful ensemble of psychological co- and cross-purposes. With the dismissal of the princes and the entrance of Lauenburg in the sham attitude of repentant Prodigal Son, king and page come together with the instrument of their destinies to play out their unconscious scripts. All three are like marionettes responding to the hidden movements of some malevolent hand. Each acts on behalf of an intention, whether his own or another's, of which he is unaware. Lauenburg does not realize that his attempt, through feigned repentance, to get close enough to the king to murder him is playing right into the latter's wish for death. While consciously accepting Lauenburg's prostration at face value ("The king raised him from the floor and enfolded him in his arms" [2:60]), on the unconscious level Gustav is well attuned to his true motives. His embrace of the man who is about to assassinate him is a kind of eerie implicit benediction of the deed. He will allow his enemy to become the vehicle of his longed-for departure from this vale of tears.

Gustel, who has been witnessing this strange reconciliation with mounting anxiety, remains trapped in the miasma of delusion, unable to see the obvious. Even in this critical moment with the king's life in the balance, and in spite of her earlier glimpse of the autonomous reality of Lauenburg's threat, she continues to project onto these antagonists aspects of her own inner conflict and is thereby rendered helpless. The king is still the idealized father and Lauenburg the doubleganger embodying the evil feminine self. The father's embrace of the doubleganger touches her deepest need to be loved by him as a woman, and she is thus moved to perceive the apparent reconciliation in these self-referential terms. The sinister motives behind Lauenburg's contrite posture are partially clouded from view as part of her dares to hope that the father is at last accepting her for what she truly is. Aberrant hope and urgent reality compete with each other for a claim on her awareness, keeping her wracked by indecision: "The men embracing seemed to float in a dizzy mist before the page's outraged eyes. *Was* this, *could* this be real? Had the king's own sanctity wrought a miracle in his depraved enemy? Or was it a diabolical trick? Was this wickedest of hypocrites deliberately befouling the purest words known? This was the way the page's doubts tumbled about, senses bewildered, temples throbbing" (2:60).

The final transaction between king and page epitomizes the tragedy of the unconscious scenario. The call to battle sounded, Gustel forces herself at the last instant to approach the king, but her approach and his response could only be described as an exercise in mutual futility. Stepping forward, she wordlessly extends the protective armor to him, which he refuses with the excuse that it is too confining:

> The page . . . started to help the king put it [the bulletproof armor] on. But the king, not at all astonished to see his page, resisted. His glance was kinder than words can describe, and he ran his fingers through Leubel-fing's curly hair as was his custom.
> "No, Gust," he said. "I don't want it. It pinches. Give me my jacket."
> (2:60)

What should be an insistent gesture of protection, made with all the persuasion at her command, is rendered mute and feeble by Gustel's delusive hope that protection is no longer necessary, that in having received the doubleganger into his arms the father has, as if in a single act of unconditional love, magically dissolved the threat of her womanhood. The reality, of course, is that in embracing Lauenburg the king had unconditionally embraced death; his refusal of the armor so tentatively offered is that of a man who does not wish to be protected. In a curious sense, the acceptance of death is all the protective armor he needs. Once having taking hold, this psychological attitude provides the one truly invulnerable armor, insulating him from all earthly concerns and filling him with a saintlike serenity that takes all events in stride. Thus, in declining the armor, he shows no surprise whatever at Gustel's sudden reappearance but simply responds to her with the deep kindness born of transcendent detachment, a kindness that she irresistibly mistakes for the long-awaited demonstration of paternal love.

Here, then, is a climactic scene in which lethal decisions—Lauenburg's to murder, the king's to *be* murdered—are put into effect that elude the awareness or control of those victimized. Neither the king, who blesses his own assassin, nor the page, who witnesses the blessing, grasps the significance of what amounts to an unconscious ritual of suicide. Each is predetermined by hidden internal forces to gloss a morbid reality. By his conscious acceptance of Lauenburg as Prodigal Son returned, the king masks from his own obstructive Protestant conscience his unconscious acceptance of Lauenburg as a weapon of suicide, while Gustel, as has been seen, is driven by unmet need to twist the king's embrace of the assassin into the father's embrace of her womanhood. Each is lost to himself and the other, each marooned on his own island of unawareness, shrouded in the opaque mists of self-deception and delusion.

Meyer puts his symbolic signature to this bleak, psychologically deterministic view of the human condition in the single-sentence paragraph with which the chapter ends: "Kurz nachher sprengte der König davon, links und rechts hinter sich den Lauenburger und seinen Pagen Leubelfing" (SW, 11:209). Twice before I have observed the use of the rider-horse image to convey the precariousness of the individual's control over the forces of unacknowledged needs and passions. That sense of precariousness is heightened here to a pitch of tragic irony as king, duke and page ride off together in model equestrian formation, to all appearances united in a common cause.

Meyer might well have chosen to end his tale here, for with the departure of the three on horseback the primary psychological narrative is over. Even though the final fifth chapter has Lauenburg actually carrying out his heinous regicide and Gustel taking a fatal bullet while valiantly attempting to deliver the slain king to secluded quarters away from the chaos of battle, these events are nevertheless anticlimactic, the inexorable physical fulfillment of predetermined psychological destinies. That Meyer considers them so is clear from the fact that he does not trouble to narrate them, but allows them to happen between chapters, as it were, thereafter simply to be reported by the secondary characters.

The author has a far more interesting and esthetically appealing purpose in mind for the final chapter, and that is to provide the tale with an ironic epilogue in which the major theme of unconscious self-deception is extended to the motley cast of surrounding characters with the implication that man's inability to face the dark, elemental side of his own nature will continue to curse him. Having brought the king's body to the parsonage of magister Tödanus with the cornet's help, Gustel now becomes the bearer of harsh truths, truths that the various characters, who find their way there one by one, willfully suppress. The brutal reality of the assassination, carried out right before her eyes, has chastened her. "Lauenburg's shot" has had the effect of a violent catharsis, sweeping in a single report the vertiginous fog of fantasy and delusion, forcing her to face, not just an earth-shattering calamity, but the unbearable knowledge that she allowed her own mind-games to prevent her from averting that calamity. One can only assume an authentic ontological guilt, a scathing sense of irredeemable personal failure, to have empowered her herculean effort, partially witnessed by the cornet, to lift the dead king onto her mount and carry him off to seclusion:[28] "The cornet spoke, choosing his words very carefully. 'I found the young man, my comrade, galloping off the battlefield and holding the king in front of him on his horse. He sacrificed his own life for His Majesty!" (2:61). The sacrifice of self indeed, but in a sense the cornet could hardly imagine. The enemy bullet Gustel had formerly wished for herself, out of a delusive guilt over the destructive power of her femininity, but which had eluded her, has finally struck her now that her guilt is legitimate. Deliberately leaving herself an open target as she spirited the victim of her "sin of omission" away, she was not long in experiencing the sudden fulfillment of her desire for atonement.

Now, as life drains from her, a sobered, enlightened Gustel struggles to set the record straight, to make her last act an unflinching testimony to a grim reality: " 'I can't die yet! I have to tell you . . .' gasped the page. 'The king . . . in the fog . . . Lauenburg's shot—' " (2:62). But death intervenes before she can clearly identify the assassin, enabling the bystanders conveniently to dismiss the obvious implication of her stammerings.

The collusive denial of an unacceptable reality by this cross-section of society—the pastor, the noble officer Ake Tott, the bourgeois merchant August Leubelfing, the cornet, and the pastor's housekeeper—lifts the theme of Gustel's individual self-deception to the level of civilized humanity in general. The individual's falsification of reality is now perpetuated by the group, even in the face of the individual's death-bed attempt to establish the truth for history. The epilogue chapter consists, then, in the tragic-ironic transposition of the deception theme from the intrapsychic to the collective social dimension.

In fact, the two major facets of the intrapsychic theme, Gustel's unconscious denial of her own femininity and her consequent blindness to Lauenburg's objective evil, recur in somber closing variations in the group's conspiracy of silence for reasons of social propriety. When an examination of Gustel's wound finally reveals her female identity, the pastor enjoins all present to secrecy, lest the king's martyrdom be tainted by sexual scandal: "I am a servant of God's Word; you are a man of gray hair, colonel; you, cornet, are an aristocrat. Mr. Laubfinger, it is to your profit and advantage. I will vouch for Mrs. Ida. We will remain silent" (2:62). It is as if the lie of sexual identity, released from Gustel's soul at the moment of death, is now free like some unchained malevolent spirit to invade the society at large. Through its silence, society will keep her lie alive. "And so I will have it [the name August Leubelfing] on your gravestone" (2:62), the pastor promises her.

A moment later, upon Gustel's passing, it is again the pastor who persuades the company to regard her disjointed but unmistakable accusation of Lauenburg as irrational rambling. The idea of the royal father's murder by one of his most distinguished sons is too repugnant to him: "The pastor, however, still with great presence of mind, was not about to have his patriotic senses [sic] besmirched by the thought that the saviour of Germany and the Protestant cause—for him one and the same thing—had fallen by the assassin hands of a German prince. He emphatically admonished them all to let this fragment of a deathbed utterance be buried with the page" (2:63). All comply in this profound dissembling of an unpalatable history, and the evildoer has now been twice protected, before the deed by Gustel's silence, after it by the group's. Once more, as in the matter of Gustel's sex, one sees the movement of the deception theme from the individual intrapsychic to the collective social sphere.

In both spheres, Lauenburg is experienced as a demonic internal force that threatens to disrupt a carefully preserved (but in reality, artificial) self-image, in the one instance of father-placating masculinity, in the other of Pan-Protestant solidarity. No less than the individual is the society driven to cover up rather than confront what it takes to be its own shadow side. Both counterfeit their own histories. The pastor, a self-committed "Diener am Wort," society's exemplar of the truthful word, leads the others in burying that word with its speaker. With this collective burial they could be said to repeat Gustel's individual act of repression on the level of society as a whole.

Gustav Adolfs Page anticipates Freud's famous dictum that repression is the price man has had to pay for civilization. Meyer knew, and helped Freud to discover, that disowned passions take refuge in the abode of the unconscious, from which they sooner or later return as demons to haunt one. The first four chapters of the tale portray this unhappy truth in the lives of the titular characters, who are, in the end, devoured by their own inner demons. The epilogue chapter, in casting a broader spotlight on society's habit of cosmeticizing its own blemishes, ominously implies the continued sovereignty of the dark denizens of the unconscious over the lives of society's future members, commoners and kings alike.

The tale ends in an image of light that is tinged with melancholy irony. The bodies of king and page are laid out together before the church altar, their reposing faces transfigured by a morning sunbeam from a nearby window: "A cloudless blue sky had followed yesterday's gloomy day, and now a ray of morning sunlight slipped through the low church window to transfigure a king's face. A tiny little beam was left over for the curly head of page Leubelfing" (2:63). This light is a deliberate allusion to those shafts of metaphysical illumination that frame the heads of saints and martyrs in the religious painting of earlier centuries. The effect is one of nostalgia for a time when men's earthly destinies, whether joyful or sad, were felt to be sanctioned by a benevolent, purposeful, infinitely wise Providence—in other words, nostalgia for the Christian world view contemporary to the characters in the work. But in symbolically commemorating an idealized world view long since called into question, this beam of light throws into stark relief the menacing darkness of the unconscious contemporary to the author's world, a darkness in which he felt compelled by intellectual and artistic honesty to shroud the destinies of his characters. Perhaps, then, the most poignant irony of all in *Gustav Adolfs Page* emerges from the shadow cast by the world view of the work over that of its characters.

In fact, this discrepancy between the kind of world the characters believe themselves to inhabit and the fictive world in which the author actually locates them gives the work a profound meta-ironic resonance. Two pervasive seventeenth-century cosmologies, the Christian and the astrological, epitomized in Gustav and Wallenstein respectively, as superseded and effectively negated by the depth-psychological model of man that was fast gaining intellectual-historical momentum at the time Meyer wrote the work. When one includes the salient features of Gustel's conscious value system in this perspective—her male chauvinism and obsessive devotion to the king—one sees that Meyer's aim is to show how the values his characters hold dear mask unconscious forces that they are unable or unwilling to confront. Put in intellectual-historical terms, his aim is to shed contemporary nineteenth-century light on seventeenth-century events, both internal and external.

This is quite in keeping with the challenge presented to the writer of historical fiction as Meyer saw it, the challenge "to permeate historical material with the life of the present."[29] As we know, Meyer formed this view of his own task from the aesthetics of Friedrich Theodor Vischer whose influential *Kritische Gänge* he had known since his youth. There Vischer says of the proper connection between historical past and present in art: "the artist might choose a scene from the past, one which would be of vital interest to contemporary trends, and thus enjoy the twofold advantage of deriving the inner substance from the intellectual world of those for whom he is writing, while deriving the forms from the past."[30] This is what Meyer has so effectively done in *Gustav Adolfs Page;* he has infused the past with the lifeblood of his own "intellectual world" and that of his educated readers.[31]

That intellectual lifeblood was largely provided by the new depth psychology that emerged in the decades before Freud with its roots variously in Darwinian biology, Schopenhauer's metaphysics, and, even further back, in the speculative psychology and natural philosophy of the early Romantics. One tends to equate depth psychology with psychoanalysis and to think of the latter as a distinctly twentieth-century phenomenon springing virtually *ex nihilo* from the mind of its Viennese founder,[32] but it is now known that most of Freud's major theories were already flourishing in philosophical garb in one or another of the various systems of *Naturphilosophie* by the time Meyer began to write fiction.[33] Darwin's *Descent of Man, and Selection in Relation to Sex* (1871) had established the view of the sexual instinct as equal in importance to survival in the regulation of all animal behavior. Before the decade ended, his work was echoed in Germany by that of the great sex-researcher, Richard von Krafft-Ebing, whose *Lehrbuch für Psychiatrie* held self-preservation and sexual gratification to be the only two instinctual aims known to physiology. This new focus on the importance of sexuality in the human sciences provided a belated sanction for earlier speculative systems of thought—most notably those of Schopenhauer, Carl Gustav Carus, and Eduard von Hartmann—that stressed the essentially pre-rational affective ground of human nature.[34] Schopenhauer was no less a pansexualist than Freud and considered the sexual instinct to overshadow even self-preservation in importance. When Schopenhauer finally came into vogue on the coattails of Darwin and the first sex-researchers, he brought the seminal concept of repression with him. For him repression was the conflict between the intellect and the instincts, which were themselves in the service of the Will; such conflict, if strong enough, could lead to insanity:[35] "The Will's opposition to let what is repellent to it come to the knowledge of the intellect is the spot through which insanity can break through into the spirit."[36] In his essay, *Freud und die Zukunft*, Thomas Mann describes the shock of recognition he experienced upon first reading Freud. Behind Freud's id and ego he recognized Schopenhauer's will and intellect and came to regard psychoanalytic concepts as Schopenhauer's ideas "translated from metaphysics into psychology."[37]

In fact, the evolution through the nineteenth century of the early Romantic notion of an immaterial dynamic force underlying all natural phenomena may be seen as a gradual transition from metaphysics to psychology. Psychiatric historian Franz Alexander speaks of a semantic shift from "will" to "unconscious mind" and sees this shift as occurring in the intellectual-historical progression from Schelling's "World Soul" through Schopenhauer's "World Will" to the highly elaborate conceptions of the individual unconscious put forward around mid-century by Carus (*Psyche*, 1846) and von Hartmann (*Philosophie des Unbewußten*, 1869).[38] In this progression the central idea of an irrational or pre-rational force is gradually (though never completely) withdrawn from the sphere of nature at large and concentrated in that of the individual psyche. Thus the metamorphosis of an idea from its original metaphysical or natural-philosophical into its "mature" psychological form. Schopenhauer, whose *Welt als Wille und Vorstellung* represents an intermediate phase in the metamorphosis in the roughly equal attention he pays to the universal Will and its individual incarnation, introduces the notion of repression in the opposition between intellect and instinct. With this, the view of the human mind, not simply as a house divided against itself, but unknowingly so, begins to take hold.[39]

These developments were solidly woven into the fabric of German intellectual life by 1882 when Meyer wrote *Gustav Adolfs Page* and, connoisseur of "die modernen philosophischen Siebensachen" that he fancied himself,[40] he was no stranger to them. Meyer's library at Kilchberg contains the 1878–79 edition of Schopenhauer's *Werke*,[41] and there is little doubt of the impact of that philosopher's notion of death as the *summum bonum*, the final release from the bondage of desire, on such characterizations as Hutten and Pescara. Nor can one help but think of the Schopenhauerian image of death as *Erlösung* (release) when one reads of Gustav Adolf's page that "her eyes flashed as she joyously rode into a hail of deadly bullets, challenging them to end her uneasy dream."

More to the point, however, is Schopenhauer's view of love as an unconscious illusion perpetuated by the Will, that is, the Will's projection onto the beloved of desirable qualities that the individual takes to be inherent in the beloved. If one reduces the cosmic conception of "Will" in Schopenhauer's speculation to the level of individual unconscious mind, one sees that it is precisely such a process that is at the basis of Gustel's fanatical devotion to the king, who becomes for her a screen of mythical dimensions upon which to project her longing for the father who has abandoned her.

To be sure, this view of love as a euphoric delusional state in which the lover transforms the beloved into an idealized object of longing is far from unique or new with Schopenhauer; it can be observed in Heinrich von Ofterdingen's dream of Mathilde and the blue flower in Novalis' *Bildungsroman* and, in its destructive aspect, in the later fiction of Hoffmann and Arnim. By the 1880s the notion of love as unconscious illusion was well established within the literary common domain. Even the tendency to locate the source of the illusion in the individual's earliest images of mother or father, such as we observe in Meyer's tale, was no longer novel by that time. One finds an imaginative rendering of the power over sexual behavior of what Freud would later call the parental *imago* as early as 1782 in Laclos's novel, *les Liaisons dangereuses,* and a superb delineation of the crippling effects of the unloving parent on the child's future love relationships in Grillparzer's *Der arme Spielmann* (1848). Nietzsche's observation that "every man bears in himself the image of his mother, and on the quality of that image will depend his future attitude to women,"[42] is the pyschological distillation of a theme already well known to literature.

Schopenhauer was not the only source of Meyer's understanding of the unconscious. One may also assume at least some familiarity on Meyer's part with the psychophilosophical theories of Eduard von Hartmann, whose *Philosophie des Unbewuβten* enjoyed an enormous vogue during the final decades of the century and probably did more to promote the notion of an unconscious mind than any other single work before Freud. Hartmann was an ardent supporter of the evolutionist thought of both Schopenhauer and

Darwin, and Freud is known to have consulted his study while writing *Die Traumdeutung*.[43] With his intellectual roots in the organic idealism of the early Romantics like Carus before him, Hartmann viewed the unconscious as a dynamic force progressing through three seamless strata ranging from the cosmic to the individual-personal: (1) the absolute unconscious, which is the irreducible stuff of the universe and the matrix for all discrete phenomena; (2) the physiological unconscious, which accounts for all organic growth in nature; (3) the psychological unconscious, which is the foundation and source of conscious mental life in man.[44]

Although interpretative studies of Hartmann's psychology have a prominent place in Meyer's library,[45] it is difficult to pinpoint specific traces of that psychology in the fiction beyond the overall intent, clearly evident, for example, in *Gustav Adolfs Page*, to mold characters motivated by unconscious forces. Meyer's published letters are of little help here, there being only one reference to Hartmann contained therein, in a letter of 15 April 1879, to Friedrich von Wyβ, in which he alludes with amusement to "Hartmann, the unconscious one," and that in a context that is not illuminating.[46] Here, as so often in Meyer's letters, the scholar is tantalized by the barest clues to the author's intellectual predilections and searches in vain for substantive elaboration. An intensely private and circumspect man, Meyer rarely allowed himself the relaxation of intellectual play, the freedom to explore ideas and work out judgments openly and at length, even within the intimate medium of the letter. One suspects that he wrote most of them with a nervous eye on posterity, and one feels compelled to say of Meyer's letters, as Thomas Mann once said of his own diaries, that they are, for an author, too often "without literary value."[47]

Nevertheless, on the basis of Meyer's demonstrable awareness at least of Hartmann's current intellectual prominence, one may speculate that a more detailed knowledge of Hartmann's ideas manifests itself in *Gustav Adolfs Page* in the name-coupling reverie into which Gustel drifts on the threshold of sleep. *Die Philosophie des Unbewußten* contains a wealth of observational data on such automatic mental functions as perception, wit, and the association of ideas, as well as considerable theorizing on the unconscious role of language in these processes.[48] Meyer, who, as has been seen, set great store by the hypnagogic state between waking and sleeping as a means of revealing his characters' innermost depths,[49] may well have been drawing on Hartmann's insights into the relationship of linguistic wit and punning to the unconscious in depicting Gustel's semiconscious play on names with its unmistakable sexual implications.

An equally probable yet elusive link between Meyer and contemporary theories of the unconscious may be found in the speculative anthropology of the great Basel jurist and scholar, Johann Jakob Bachofen. Bachofen's *Das Mutterrecht. Eine Untersuchung über die Gynaekokratie der alten Welt nach ihrer religiösen und rechtlichen Natur* (1861) suggests itself as an intriguing possible source for the particular structure of Gustel's sexual-identity conflict. On the basis of the symbolic implications of antique art and mythology, this study proposed the theory, so unsettling to the contemporary male-dominated bourgeois society, that the present-day patriarchal culture was not an eternal, immutable phenomenon of Western history, but had actually been preceded by an era of matriarchy whose origin more or less coincided with the advent of agriculture and the building of towns. Female domination in this prehistoric culture, argued Bachofen, extended beyond the pragmatic spheres of politics, kinship systems, and social relations to the broader reaches of religion and *Weltanschauung*. Virtually every facet of the culture was informed by the female principle. The supreme value placed on fertility was reflected in the universal reverence for the procreative powers of women, as well as in the sovereign position held by women in the individual family, the definition of matricide as the most heinous of all crimes, and the worship of Ceres, goddess of the harvest, as the premiere divinity.[50]

Bachofen regarded the historical transition from matriarchy to patriarchy as an evolution to a higher stage of civilization, occurring over a long period of bitter struggle. In the new order the value previously placed on motherhood is now accorded fatherhood. Love of the father is seen as a higher, more spiritualized emotion, superseding the more material, biological bond between mother and child. Whereas matriarchy fostered dependency, patriarchy favors autonomy and provides the cultural context for a more refined state of individual self-realization. Once the patriarchal culture had sunk its roots, the memory of the preceding matriarchal order supposedly became anathema to it. This hateful memory was gradually "erased" through a process of collective forgetting, leaving behind only vague, oblique traces in the symbols and myths of the patriarchal culture.[51]

Although Bachofen's ideas find no forum in Meyer's letters, the theory of matriarchy could hardly have escaped his attention, inasmuch as the controversy aroused by the work of this fellow Swiss had begun to spread beyond the borders of Switzerland by the 1880s. Also, Meyer's personal acquaintance with Bachofen on the occasion of the former's purchase of the Kilchbert property on Lake Zurich is recorded by Frey. It seems that the two men had waged a bidding war for the property from which Meyer eventually emerged victorious. In a letter to his sister Betsy of 18 January 1877, he could finally make the happy announcement, "It is now decided. Yesterday the Otto property became ours. Last joust with the rich Baseler Bachofen."[52]

It seems a distinct possibility that Bachofen's reconstruction of an ancient matriarchal order that had been overthrown and "collectively repressed" by the succeeding male-dominated culture gave Meyer the germ of an idea for Gustel's characterization. Meyer may well have telescoped Bachofen's vision of cultural-historical process down to the level of his heroine's individual conflict-ridden development. As has been seen, Gustel's interior history is essentially the repression of the feminine by the masculine principle in conformity to the implicit dictates of the love-withholding father. Gustel's identification with the misogynous masculine principle, her "masculinity complex" in Horney's term, parallels Bachofen's view of the racial subjugation of women in the patriarchal society.

Nor should such creative borrowing on Meyer's part surprise us, for although this transposition of a seminal idea from the level of racial to that of individual, and fictitious, history is certainly to be viewed as an ingenious act of the poetic imagination, it was in no sense an intellectual anomaly. Similar creative transpositions from the "macro" to the "micro" sphere were occurring on many intellectual fronts from the mid-nineteenth century onward. The biological principle that ontogeny recapitulates phylogeny in the embryonic gestation of the individual organism was well entrenched by Meyer's time. I have also noted above the gradual relocation of the early Romantic notion of a cosmic vital force within the individual psyche under its new name, "the unconscious," in the systems of the philosopher-psychologists, Carus and Hartmann. Moreover, although Meyer may have been the first, he was not the only thinker to telescope Bachofen's theories of racial evolution to the individual sphere. Ellenberger observes many parallels between Bachofen's anthropology and Freud's theories of individual psycho-sexual development and points to Bachofen as the source of Adler's contention "that the present oppression of women by men was an overcompensation of the male against a previous stage of female domination. . . . the neurotic, being handicapped by a fear of women, develops within himself a 'virile protest,' so that he is, in his neurosis, the plaything of that struggle between the male and female principles."[53] Insofar as Gustel Leubelfing unconsciously sets herself the life-task of remaking herself in the image of her father, one could say that this foredoomed struggle within her between the male and female principles is the father's tragic legacy to her.

All his life Meyer clung to strong, independent women[54]—the mother who almost singlehandedly held the family together upon the father's early death,[55] the sister who gave him endless encouragement and assistance in his work and helped him through bouts of severe depression, the score of professional women like Cecile Borrel, Eliza Wille, Betty Paoli, and Louise von Frànçois, who supported him at one critical juncture or another in both his personal and artistic growth. One might therefore expect the notion of a primordial matriarchy to have held some fascination, some mythical plausibility for him; one might further expect his perception of the domestic bondage in his own culture of gifted women like his mother, a bondage reinforced by women's largely unquestioning acceptance of male primacy, to have found its way, however circuitously, into the fiction. The closest visual prototype of Gustel from Meyer's own era would probably have been the notorious George Sand, whose works the poet had read in his youth.[56] But whereas Gustel's transvestitism, like her cultivation of male habits and predilections generally, must be read as a sign of her unconscious victimization by her father's male chauvinism, Sand's waistcoat, trousers, and fragrant panatella were the deliberate, aggressive symbols of protest against that chauvinism. Perhaps Meyer, in conceiving Gustel, imaginatively turned the historical clock back on Sand's sexual-political activism, envisioning his seventeenth-century heroine's donning of male attire as the very act of unconscious surrender to sexist tyranny that Sand would later raise to the level of conscious rebellion.

Gustel's unconscious attempt to become a man represents what Freud and Horney would later identify as a perversion of normal Oedipal strivings. Since she cannot win the misogynous father's love as a woman, she will do so by becoming a man. The association of childhood sexuality with the Oedipus myth was Freud's original invention, and the idea of Gustel's frustrated love for her father taking a deviant, pathological turn, ending in transference to the king as ideal father, was probably Meyer's own. However, the theory of childhood sexuality itself was quite widespread in the latter half of the nineteenth century, although more so among educators and clergy than among physicians. Ake Tott's conclusion, upon learning of Gustel's zealous devotion to the king who had fondled her in infancy, that "you shouldn't kiss little children. Kisses like that can sleep and then burst into flame when lips are fuller and more ready for them" could be found as a common admonition to parents in many of the popular educational manuals that appeared in Meyer's day. Moral theologians warned of the dangers of infantile masturbation, sex-play among children, and the seduction of young children by servants. It was believed that any display of sexuality by a child could lead to the acquisition of "bad habits" that might yield bitter fruit in later years.[57]

One of these educators, Jules Michelet, was well known to Meyer from his powerfully visionary treatises on French history.[58] Much more popular among the reading public, however, were Michelet's works on education, one of which, Nos Fils (1869), contains most of the seminal ideas that Freud would eventually synthesize into his theory of the Oedipus complex. Children, Michelet argued, were sexually inclined from birth, and parents should take care not to stimulate their amorous instincts. The small child had a natural, intense jealousy of the same-sex parent and often simulated sleep in order to spy on his parents' intimate behavior. Michelet especially stressed the relevance of the ancient Jewish writings that adjured fathers to keep a safe distance from their daughters.[59] It is not known whether Meyer was as well acquainted with Michelet's theories on child-rearing as he was with his historical writings, which themselves, incidentally, hypothesized the crucial role of unconscious forces, the operation of a subliminal collective spirit of

Jeanne d'Arc, in the evolution of French society.[60] but it would not be rash to assume such an acquaintance, just as it would only be prudent to assume a confluence in Meyer's imagination of some of these popular caveats regarding childhood sexuality during the working-out of Gustel's character—and, more specifically, during the working-out of Ake Tott's view of that character.

In donning her father's uniform, Gustel is unconsciously assuming a mask, a façade of masculinity meant to conceal her rejected feminine identity from herself and others. Meyer has been dubbed by Louis Wiesmann "the poet of the mask," and one might picture the critical reader of *Gustav Adolfs Page* as a kind of psychological detective whose job it is to interpret the various features of Gustel's mask as clues to the "dark psychological processes"—to borrow Frey's phrase for Meyer's authorial predilection[61]—that lie behind it. Meyer's tale belongs to the inchoate surge of an intellectual-historical wave that Ellenberger aptly calls an " 'unmasking' trend, that search for hidden unconscious motivations characteristic of the 1880s and 1890s."[62] The unflinching pursuit of an abhorrent truth underlying the deception of self and others became an almost obsessive concern of philosophy, social criticism, and literature during this period. It is no exaggeration to say that Meyer was steeped in an intellectual culture for which simple human benevolence itself had become suspect. The tentative Christian faith he had managed to salvage from that first shattering encounter with Vischer's realist aesthetics must have been sorely tested many times over by the array of seductive iconoclasts who crossed his path during his productive decades.[63] As has been seen, by the time he came to write *Gustav Adolfs Page*, Meyer had read Schopenhauer, who had unmasked romantic love as the cloying strategem of a blindly procreative cosmic force; a few years later he would be pondering the acid social analysis of Max Nordau, whose popular books viewed modern civilization as a fabric of lies and deceit,[64] and he would be brushing up against Nietzsche's *Jenseits von Gut und Böse*, which had presumed to strip Christian conscience down to its naked essence as warped aggression.[65] What have since become the complementary deities of modern depth psychology, sex and aggression, were launching their relentless assault on the paternal, still Pietistically tinged God of Meyer's maturity, their growing hegemony clearly manifest in the author's melancholy admission that he had "trust in God, as much as a child of the nineteenth century can have." The Joan of Schiller's prologue at the century's turn and the Gustel of Meyer's tale some eighty years later, each conceived as in bondage to the Omnipotent Father, measure the progress of a demythologizing juggernaut gathering momentum along its inexorable path towards Freud's confident pronouncement that God was no more than the image of the father cast across the sky.

Much of the European literature roughly contemporary to *Gustav Adolfs Page* was experimenting with the now-commonplace models of mind as glacier or archipelago whose familiar surface contours belie a vast submerged mass of uncharted shapes and forces. One thinks here especially of the newly prominent Russo-Nordic wave of Dostoyevsky, Ibsen, and Strindberg, all authors with whose work Meyer either already was or would soon become familiar. But even closer to home, from that earlier psychological tour de force, Otto Ludwig's *Zwischen Himmel und Erde*, Meyer must have learned much about the dark phantasms of lust, revenge and guilt that lurk behind the fragile structures of ordered life; and his terse description of that novel in 1874 as "ein peinliches Buch" is, I think, to be taken in the sense of "painstakingly analytical" or "exhaustive," the more so in view of his later judgment of Ludwig's plays as "too reflective."[66] Meyer's reservations about Ludwig's novel did not concern the validity of the latter's focus on his characters' psychopathology but rather the style of narration of that pathology, which was, for his taste, far too clinically discursive. For Meyer the narrator's role was not to analyze his characters' mental life but to imply it through the revelation of salient details of external behavior and the condensed symbolic action of dreams. The labored, *durchdachte* quality of Ludwig's psychology, in implied contrast to his own light-handed intimation of the interior world, is emphasized in Meyer's letter of September 1875 to Lingg, in which he grants Ludwig's dramatic characters the status of "quite lively, rounded individuals," an accomplishment wrought, however, "with hands tired and palsied by effort."[67]

Meyer had no such misgivings about another psychological novel, Dostoyevsky's *Crime and Punishment*. An unabashed admiration for the Russian's brilliant dissection of the remorse-ridden conscience is evident in his description of the novel as "most worth reading, a morbid masterpiece (though still ranking high above Zola), from which a healthy person can learn an endless amount (i.e., can actually study anatomy)."[68] While it is true that Meyer's only known references to Dostoyevsky occur in two letters to François Wille of 18 and 30 March 1885, this does not preclude the possibility of his having read the novel earlier and having pondered, in the self-professed posture of a student, the psychic "anatomy" of the tormented young murderer, Raskolnikov, in fashioning the theme of Gustel's guilt over imagined parricide. Certainly his remark to Wille in the first letter, "Meanwhile I'm studying Dostoyevsky," could be taken to imply an earlier reading followed now by a more careful scrutiny.[69]

While the question of literary influences on Meyer's grasp of depth psychology must remain largely a matter of speculation, there can be no question of that grasp itself. Quite apart from the internal textual evidence of *Gustav Adolfs Page*, remarks scattered here and there throughout the correspondence enable one to piece together the picture of a mature, almost elegant understanding of the notion of an unconscious mind. This understanding may be traced at least as far back as his letter of December 1877 to

Friedrich von Wyβ in which he discusses his *modus operandi* with respect to prospective literary subjects: "Beyond this, I practically think my new materials to death, in anticipation of the moment when, having fully thought them through, I can turn myself over to instinct, which is always the best guide in such matters."[70]

This passage, in which Meyer stresses his reliance, well before any actual writing, on a process of unconscious gestation for the growth and elaboration of a fictive idea, has two features in common with all his utterances on the unconscious: its designation of the phenomenon by the term *Instinct* rather than *das Unbewuβte* (the unconscious) and its view of such instinct as a positive and autonomous creative force. With respect to the first of these, the absence of such terms as *unbewuβt* and *das Unbewuβte* from Meyer's description of indeliberate or automatic processes is not at all surprising, inasmuch as these expressions had not yet become part of even the educated person's active vocabulary. Although Carus had inaugurated the term *das Unbewuβte* in 1846 and Hartmann had promulgated both the term and the concept in the 1870s, and even long before either, in 1807, the Romantic physicist Johann Ritter had described the mind of a hypnotized subject as "eines passiven Bewuβtseins,"[71] still it was not until Freud and Jung achieved stature early in this century that the term moved into general usage. Before this, automatic processes, especially those having to do with artistic creation, were commonly characterized as *instinktiv* or by the Schillerian *naiv.* Thus Meyer, in a letter to François Wille, speaks of Wagner's genius as having "einer unzerstörbar-naiven u. kindlichen Seite."[72] That he is referring here to a capacity in Wagner that today might be described by psychologists as endopsychic or unconscious is clear from the phrase that follows: "neben sehr bewuβten Absichten."

The other feature that runs through all Meyer's pronouncements on the unconscious—the stress on its artless, effortless creativity—is interesting from an aesthetic-historical point of view, reflecting as it does the continued vitality of the Romantic vision of artistic creativity as a most natural process, indeed, as a manifestation of nature in its most highly evolved state. The following lines, from a letter of December 1885 to Carl Spitteler, show how much Meyer's artistic self-perception retains in common with the organic aesthetics of Goethe and the early Romantics. Common to all is the belief that the artist, especially in the conception and early genesis of his work, must surrender in trust to inner purposive processes that are grounded in nature and that operate beyond his direct observation or control: "a dominant factor in my works is the length of time (3, 5 or 10 years) during which my imagination is occupied with them, completely without effort, though continuously: vegetatively, as it were, though still with latent intelligence, just as it should be. Doesn't nature at large also create in this instinctive-teleological manner?"[73] The close resemblance between this psychologistic view of human creativity to which Meyer subscribed and the early Romantic image of the artist as attuned to the blind but intrinsically intelligent forces of nature will not surprise us if we bear in mind that Meyer stands on the shoulders of the mid-century philosopher-psychologists, Hartmann and Carus, whose theories extend the speculative *Naturphilosophie* of the romantics into the realm of the human psyche.

But what is most curious about these scattered remarks of Meyer's on the unconscious is that they contain not a single reference, direct or indirect, to the pathological sphere. Nothing of the chaos of feeling, the madness of idea or attitude that sometimes festers behind the façade of rationality. Nothing of the invisible shaping influence of the repressed. In short, nothing of the themes that work so powerfully in *Gustav Adolfs Page*. Meyer's emphasis in the letters on the sunny cooperation between conscious and unconscious designs in the creative process would seem to make him more proto-Jungian than Freudian. When voicing a personal opinion, he anticipates more closely the optimistic, mandala-bound teleology of his fellow Zuricher than the grim determinism of the Viennese master. His own artistry he views rather as an organismic response to future possibilities than an end-product of influences from an irretrievable past.

How to explain such a disparity between the bold exploration of the destructive unconscious in the fiction and the exclusive focus on the creative unconscious in the letters? Perhaps the question becomes a little less vexing when one recalls the many critics who have characterized Meyer the artist as something of an alter ego to Meyer the man. Bridgwater is among those more recent commentators who, by implication at least, interpret Meyer's art as symbolic compensation for the intense, passionate living denied him by the encumbrance of a phlegmatic, primly conservative character. Thus, for example, "as a man Meyer will have rejected Nietzsche's ideal of *Vornehmheit*, and yet he personally embodied it and shared it as a *poetic* view (cp. his aesthetic admiration of the amoral power-seekers whom he condemned morally)."[74] It would seem that Meyer maintained a discreet reticence with respect to certain contemporary ideas that he found exciting but that happened to be alien to his Protestant moral character. However, such ideas, though blocked from direct expression, would often find their way into the fiction where they were lavishly entertained. The image of man as a creature doomed by his own unawareness endlessly to reenact the failed primal relationships of his past with present-time surrogates repulsed the Christian—even one on intimate terms with the Calvinist doctrine of predestination—but intrigued the artist as a potentially rich vein of tragic narrative.

On controversial ideas, then, Meyer generally let his fiction speak for him. The demonic, double-edged nature of the unconscious as he surely understood it, its capacity to create or destroy, to fulfill or enslave, to generate form or unleash violence, was not a subject he could ever have felt at ease to discuss. Then too, when one notes that all his comments on the unconscious in the letters occur, not in the abstract, but in a personal context of artistic self-analysis, one realizes how less likely still he would have been to broach the dark side of the phenomenon on this sensitive ground. In his correspondence Meyer operated, as previously noted, within very rigid bounds of self-imposed censorship, and clearly the subject of strictest censorship was he himself. While he might indulge in some occasional safe and self-congratulatory speculation on the creative contribution of his own unconscious to the working-out of a narrative form, he would never have openly explored, say, the possible role of unconscious factors in his youthful bouts with depression or in the severe nervous breakdown to which these ultimately led at the age of twenty-seven.[75] The matter of his own inner demons Meyer was wont to pass over in silence, with the exception of those occasions when they could be prevailed upon to act with him rather than against him.

If, against all odds, one still wishes to pin Meyer down on the issue of the unconscious as a potential Pandora's Box, to secure at least a scrap of extratextual evidence for his awareness of the precarious balance of its energies, one must content oneself with an inference to be drawn from a letter of June 1891 to Joseph Widmann. Here again one finds him remarking on the automatic, instinctive aspect of his own narrative composing: "I'm just now finishing up another novella *[Angela Borgia]* and, I must say, I feel a bit queer about it, a bit strange. You wouldn't believe how instinctively I usually work, giving the horse free rein and letting it seek its way. My strong sense of composition—as G. Keller termed it midway between blame and praise—and my particularly contrived effects must be in my blood. Really, who knows himself?!"[76] The image of the horse assuming control from the rider will by now have become a staple of our discussion. In its first occurrence, in Gustel's dream, it warned in proto-Freudian terms of the ego's unwitting surrender to the unbridled passions of the id. Here the poet uses it to describe rather a deliberate self-surrender to his own unconscious energies toward a benign, constructive end. The conscious nature of this intentional relinquishing of control over the creative process guarantees the poet's retention of a degree of passive control, a kind of overseeing or supervisory function, analogous perhaps to Gustel's giving the horse its own head during her frantic flight from camp. But Meyer must have sensed such control to be fragile indeed. It is recalled that even Gustel's well-intentioned flight was based on a magical delusion, namely, that her presence was lethal to the king. Who would presume to judge at what point passive control becomes loss of control? When does "going with the flow," even the flow of creativity, become "being swept up by the flood"? When do the reins turn from a guiding device into a means of holding on? Surely the essential meaning of the rider-horse image for Meyer is this very tension of instability, this flirtation with chaos, that marks man's relationship to his own hidden powers of creation. This is the inference to be drawn from his use of a single supple image to express contrary meanings, both his own actualization as an artist and his heroine's imminent psychic collapse. Such an image conveys more indelibly than even the most eloquent exposition ever could Meyer's subtle appreciation of the demonic nature of the unconscious.

Let it stand, then, as the fitting emblem of a tale that portrays the demonic unconscious in what is perhaps its most tragic manifestation, the perversion of sexual identity. Even though written in an era defined by its obsession with psychic masks, *Gustav Adolfs Page* probes this most elusive of themes with a depth of discernment one would have thought unattainable before psychoanalysis. The heed paid Meyer by the father of that movement would seem to have been well-founded indeed.

3

Unconsciousness in Terms of Lapsarian Myth in *Das Leiden eines Knaben*

IN 1806 Kleist wrote wistfully to a friend, "Any first movement, anything involuntary, is beautiful, but becomes twisted and perverse the instant it comprehends itself."[1] Spontaneity seeing itself and, in the act of seeing, self-destructing: this was Kleist's particular formulation of the Fall from Grace, his version of the primal myth of Romanticism. Four years later he would elaborate his reflection in that brilliant meditation on the vicissitudes of human consciousness, "Über das Marionettentheater."

Some seventy-three years after that, Meyer would write a novella, *Das Leiden eines Knaben*, which, for all its realism of historical personage and narrative technique, had something very much like this Kleistian Romantic vision of the Fall as its mythical subtext. In Meyer's tale the manifest theme of the young innocent brutalized by a society obsessed with power and status is grounded in an expansive stratum of myth, a latent terrain of commingled biblical and Romantic imagery. It is a tragic terrain for which Kleist's reflection could serve as a map, one in which spontaneity fatally succumbs to self-awareness, natural movement to studied gesture, direct sight to gnarled projection. On the mythic level, *Das Leiden eines Knaben* is about the burden of corruption borne by human society from the instant man took himself as an object. It is the Fall from Grace according to Meyer.

In these pages I will explore Meyer's careful weaving of the lapsarian myth through the major themes and characters of *Das Leiden eines Knaben*.[2] As I do so, it will become clear that the relations between the historically specific and the mythic dimensions of the tale form a web so seamless, and hence so rich in poetic texture, as to constitute Meyer's ultimate artistic expression of the unconscious idea.

I say "the unconscious idea" because the Fall from Grace is conceived here (just as in Kleist's essay) as a fall from consciousness into unconsciousness, that is, from an open, Edenic condition of "seeing," in which the dualism of "I" and "not-I" has not yet been recognized, into a closed, solipsistic condition of "being seen," in which it has.[3] Man's capacity to abstract himself, to conceive of himself as separate from the rest of creation, raises him above the beasts and defines his evolutionary advance on them. But the power of self-reflection, as Kleist and the other Romantics never tired of reminding us, is an ambiguous power that exacts a heavy toll, for it is only gained at the expense of unity, the unity that alone exists when one is lost, as it were, in direct apprehension of the other, when one is "seeing" rather than "being seen." *Das Leiden eines Knaben* takes up the Romantic melancholy over this loss of naive unity and vision and, echoing the earlier movement, shows man's vaunted self-consciousness to be a form of blindness, a lethal egocentrism that casts him out of a timeless Eden into the time-bound prisons of history and society. Once man holds up the mirror, he essentially ceases to "see" and experiences predominantly "being seen" or "seenness." This isolating experience of seenness is a mortal unconsciousness of the spirit; it is the Original Sin and constitutes man's Fall from Grace ("And they became aware of their nakedness" [Gen. 3 : 7]).

In *Das Leiden eines Knaben* unconsciousness qua self-consciousness— that is, seenness—is portrayed as a state of psychological and spiritual exile giving rise to all those brutalizing relations of power among men to which is given the name "society." The members of the court society in Meyer's tale are habitually, irredeemably self-conscious. They behave in ways calculated to win the approval of a sometimes real, but more often imagined judge, authority figure, or even vaguely transpersonal observing spirit. Those who surround the throne of Louis XIV, and even the throne's occupant himself, have in various ways relinquished their power of sight—their consciousness—to someone or something else, so that that power is now turned as a weapon against them. Since they no longer "see" but, conversely, experience themselves as "seen," they can be said to have become unconscious. They are the unconscious society.

Some discussion of a scene that occurs about midway in the tale will quickly lend flesh and blood to this unpardonably abstract statement of my thesis. The scene in question has the salty Countess Mimeure expressing her concern to Fagon, as the latter recounts it to the king and Maintenon in the frame, about the social plight of Mirabelle and Julian during a promenade through the royal botanical garden. The two children are also strolling together in this "Paradiese" (*SW*, 12 : 132) just a few yards ahead of them:

"Wie schlank sie schreiten!" flüsterte die Alte hinter den sich Entfernenden. "Adam und Eva! Lache nicht, Fagon! Ob das Mädchen Puder und

Reifrock trägt, wandeln sie doch im Paradiese, und auch unschuldig sind sie, weil eine leidenvolle Jugend auf ihnen liegt und sie die reine Liebe empfinden läßt, ohne den Stachel ihrer Jahre." (SW, 12:132)

Mimeure romanticizes the tender relationship of the hapless youths, for whom she feels a special affection and responsibility, by casting them in the roles of the innocent first inhabitants of Eden. Their mutual suffering in the corrupt world outside the Garden has kept their love pure, preserving it from the normal desires of puberty ("den Stachel ihrer Jahre"). Fagon, of course, finds Mimeure's Genesis scenario a bit overdone and tells her as much through his laughter. Undaunted, the countess continues to spin out the Edenic metaphor, focusing now on Mirabelle's double life, in and outside this Paradise Parisian style.

Placing various motifs of the Edenic/lapsarian myth in the mouths of his characters, most of whom, like Mimeure, are articulate, educated Christians and hence conversant with them, is one of Meyer's primary means of elaborating the mythical subtext. Fagon's good-natured scoffing provides just the right muting note to keep the subtext from appearing too overtly melodramatic in Mimeure's version. When Meyer speaks for himself, he can be subtle; when he speaks through the feisty Mimeure, subtlety must be replaced by her listener's benign derision.

Mimeure goes on to describe Mirabelle's childhood, and we learn that it was in another garden that the girl lost her innocence. The "fallen" Mirabelle, the girl who suffers the tortures of a paralyzing self-consciousness in court society, has become a prisoner of the over-inflated rhetoric she employs in order to appear intelligent to others. It is an absurdly formal manner of speaking, the outdated style of the *précieuse*, which she learned from her mother, "the vicomtesse," who entertained the Dijon gentry in "a regular garden of poetry . . . with all the circumlocutions and the fancy forms of the late Mademoiselle de Scudéry" (2:87).

As the tool of self-consciousness, language is thus implicated in the Fall from Grace. The expulsion from Paradise is the necessary consequence of man's perversion of the natural function of language to name and represent things. In Mirabelle's case, language has become, as Mimeure puts it, "dieser garstige Höcker" (this loathsome hump) (SW, 12:132), for it no longer serves simply to identify the things she sees; rather she has perverted—or inverted—language, i.e., turned it inward on herself to cosmeticize a poor self-image. She is terrified of being perceived by others as stupid and cultivates rhetoric as a counterfeit intelligence. Her painful self-consciousness, an obsessive preoccupation with how she "comes across" at court, is the inversion, and hence *per*version, of her original power of sight and the correlative power to name what she sees. She is incapable of meeting Fagon as Fagon, but must inflate him into the "first man among physicians and scientists"

(2 : 85). In vain Mimeure tries through gentle ridicule to help her deflect her language from this grotesque, self-aggrandizing solipsism (it is really herself she is aggrandizing, not Fagon) back to its natural function of calling people and things what they are: "This man is not 'the first among physicians,' but simply Mr. Fagon. The botanical garden is nothing but the botanical garden or the herb garden or the royal garden. Paris is Paris and not 'the capital,' and the king is quite content to be just the king. Remember that the next time" (2 : 86).[4]

Mirabelle's Original Sin is thus conceived as a lapse from the pristine powers of seeing and naming that Eve at first enjoyed in the Garden into the sightlessness of self-awareness, the experience of being named or labeled. The lapse from seeing and labeling into being seen and being labeled is a lapse from consciousness into unconsciousness.

One sees then, from Mimeure's quasi-mythical characterization of Mirabelle, that the Fall only becomes possible with the genesis of language. With language man gains the capacity to symbolize or represent things in awareness. From there it is but a short step to symbolizing oneself as a discrete entity and holding a verbal image or idea of this so-conceived separate self-entity in the mind. Man's image of himself becomes his most precious possession, to be defended and enhanced at all costs, even at the cost of a direct, loving apprehension of the world around him, even at the cost of Paradise.

During her occasional visits with Julian in the Garden, Mirabelle can briefly return to innocence. As Mimeure surmises, "I'll bet she's now talking quite naturally with him. Her soul is simple, her spirit is pure" (2 : 88). But once outside the Garden in society, she unfailingly becomes aware of her "nakedness" ("her simple nature") and hastens to cover this exposure of self with the fig leaf of rhetoric ("these rag-patchwork phrases" [2 : 88]). The terms of the lapsarian metaphor are, again, Mimeure's. Indeed, she weaves the motifs of the myth into her description of Mirabelle's plight with a poetic skill that, in this passage at least, is certainly more Meyer's than her own: "But whenever she attends a morning social with me and is seated next to some big name, an archbishop or a duke, then she's frightened to death of seeming stupid or empty-headed. Fear makes her bedeck her simple nature with these rag-patchwork phrases" (2 : 88).

Like Mirabelle, albeit not as overtly, most of the members of this court society suffer the oppressive sense of being watched by a powerful judging presence.[5] Like her, they are, in one sense or another, "aware of their nakedness," fallen creatures. Rather than seeing the world and creatively acting upon it, they are seen and acted upon by it, manipulated by the compulsion to appear favorably in the sight of the watching power—or at least to avoid its censure. Mimeure herself is a good example. For years she has stayed away from Versailles for fear of offending the king's delicate aesthetic sensibilities with the wrinkles and sagging flesh of her age. She pities Mirabelle for her feelings of intellectual and social inferiority, but is herself gripped by a painful obsession with her own physical imperfections that has severely narrowed her sphere of social influence, so much so, in fact, that she has not been able to muster the courage to intercede with the king on Julian's behalf. She is never completely free of the feeling of being seen as ugly and tries to compensate with spicy language and an aggressive, earthy manner that pretends to spurn all formality. But from some remote corner of her imagination Louis the aesthete is forever watching her, studying her as a curiosity, all the while shielding himself from her "offensiveness" with upheld perfumed handkerchief.

Still in the same scene, Meyer presents, through Fagon's recollection, a symbolic picture of Mimeure's painful experience of seenness. It is one of those visually arresting *tableaux vivantes* to which the author so often has recourse in adumbrating character relationships and themes. Reduced to walking laboriously with a cane, Mimeure looks for a comfortable seat in the garden from which to continue her chat with Fagon. They happen upon a bench behind which sits a bust of the king mounted on a pedestal: " 'Ooof!' wheezed the countess, tired from hobbling along on her cane, as she sat down heavily on a stone bench. It was the one in the rondeau of myrtle and laurel, Sire, where your bust is located" (2:88). It is clear from Fagon's account that Mimeure cannot quite free her mind from that ominous sculpted "presence" right behind her, even in the midst of her heated expression of concern for Mirabelle and Julian, for she concludes her lament with a pointed reference to it: " 'Mark my words, Fagon, Julian is now my adopted son, and if you don't get him released from the Jesuits and provide him with a proper life, then by all that's holy, I'll hobble my way to Versailles and in spite of all my wrinkles I'll take up the matter with *him!*' With that she pointed to your bust with its laurel wreath, Majesty" (2:88–89). This *tableau* is especially rich in thematic suggestiveness, creating as it does the graphically ironic image of one character bemoaning the ills of excessive shyness in another at the very moment she is herself squirming nervously under the piercing gaze of the imagined presence behind her. Mimeure's observation of self-consciousness in Mirabelle and Julian is framed by her own nagging dis-ease over being watched. Through the irony of this "vertical" hierarchy of seenness, Meyer's *tableau* generates a powerful sense of the ubiquity of man's fallen state.

This scene is a good point of departure for the ensuing discussion of *Das Leiden eines Knaben,* for it provides a concise exposition of the main thematic terms of the mythical subtext: the Fall from the bliss of primal consciousness into the suffering endemic to self-aware, hence unconscious, man; from the spontaneous flow and movement of seeing into the creeping paralysis of being seen; from the botanical garden as timeless Eden to the court as society embedded in history. Putting it in terms of the tale's inner form, one might say that the subtext is structured along an axis that bisects pre- and post-lapsarian conditions, the former largely identifiable in a spatio-symbolic sense with the communal botanical garden, the latter with the court as the aggregate of an exiled human society. From the vantage point established by the discussion of this middle scene, we can now look backward and forward in the text to discover how the major characters and events of the tale's historical dimension "fit into" the mythical structure. In so doing, we will soon come to savor the poetic power that accrues to the historical tale by virtue of this subtle, but pervasive resonance of myth.

Where better to begin than in the Garden, where the myth itself begins. One notes that, although Louis XIV at one time decreed the construction and cultivation of a royal botanical garden, he has apparently taken little notice of it since. The garden has, in a sense, become more Fagon's turf than his ever since he set the physician up in a modest dwelling there to reward him for his long years of service. Fagon reminds the king of his long-standing but unkept promise to visit his chemical laboratory ("a good-sized chemical laboratory that you have promised me to visit someday" [2:77]), situated in the garden's north end, from which one infers that the king has been too busy with affairs of state to take time out for refreshment amidst the quickening verdant fragrances of this urban oasis. But then it is learned that there are others for whom the garden is even more a home than for Fagon. There is in fact a modest garden community that has gradually formed around him, a small group of social misfits at whose disposal he has placed the garden as a casual retreat from the bustle of the surrounding metropolis. This community consists of the backward Julian, entrusted to Fagon's care by his mother on her deathbed, the vagrant painter Mouton, and Mouton's poodle, which the painter, with characteristic eccentricity, has named after himself.

Fagon tells the king of the pleasant company provided by his "three guests. I call them my guests because Julian Boufflers, whom I am telling you about, Mouton the man, and Mouton the dog often spent many contented hours with me" (2:81). One is struck by Fagon's singling-out of the dog as "the most gifted" of the three: "Dieser zweite Mouton . . . war ohne Zweifel—in den Schranken seiner Natur—der begabteste meiner drei Gäste" (SW, 12:122–23). The surface thrust of Fagon's remark is obviously facetious, but that very facetiousness, directed as it uncharacteristically is against his own ward, cues one to look for a deeper sense in "der begabteste," a sense that even Fagon himself does not fully grasp. Other details in his description of the dog bring quick disclosure, for instance, his introduction of "Mouton Number Two" into his story as "an intelligent poodle with a large brain and very intelligent eyes" (2:81). Moments later, he recollects a charming interlude in which he observed Mouton from his library window giving Julian a painting lesson in the attic of the adjacent building: "Mouton the poodle was sitting on a tall red-cushioned chair next to them, looking intelligent and knowledgeable, as though he had only the highest regard for this fine entertainment" (2:82). Deciding to join the congenial group, Fagon recalls entering the attic: "The happy artists couldn't hear me as I entered in my felt slippers. Only Poodle Mouton noticed me" (2:82). Taken together, these qualities of the dog's "giftedness"—a certain wisdom, a large head suggesting intelligence, knowing eyes, powers of sensation beyond the ordinary human range, an unmistakable attitude of unreserved benevolence—point to a very special animal indeed. They suggest an original denizen of the Garden, the embodiment of an Edenic consciousness that grasps its natural surroundings with the immediacy of a loving embrace, without a trace of the filter of conceptual thought or discriminating judgment, the hallmarks of self-conscious man. In this sense Mouton the poodle *is* "der begabteste"; he is sovereign over all he surveys and may be said to "reign" over the Garden at large. Hence his regal pose as Fagon conveys it here, "enthroned" as he is "on a tall red-cushioned chair," beaming royal approval of the creative activity of his two human "subjects."

Without deliberately intending it, Fagon is here leveling against Louis a subtle critique of his monarchy by alluding to a natural style of kingship totally at odds with his. In the dog's kingdom Julian once flourished; in that of Louis XIV he has perished. The subtlety of Fagon's implicit comparison is totally lost on Louis, but not on the reader, who at this point begins to grasp the significance of the botanical garden as a quasi Eden, a paradisiacal kingdom whose three inhabitants (Fagon's place in the Garden is problematic and will be taken up later) live in harmony with each other and their environment.

In various places the text invites us to extrapolate on the basis of this understanding of Mouton the poodle as "der begabteste." Earmarks of Eden, and of the blissful, inviolate consciousness that is its essence, abound. If the dog is "Master" of the Garden by virtue of his perfectly effortless apprehension of nature, a kind of direct sight that is synonymous with love, which is in turn synonymous with unity, then Mouton and Julian are by the same token his "apprentices." To the extent that they are self-conscious beings, they belong to the Fallen race of man, but this is decidedly their lesser part, for they enjoy a high degree of the direct sight of the animal, occasionally glimpsing Paradise, and so can be "apprenticed" to the dog as painters. Painting is the apprenticeship, the *Bildung* or "genialen Tätigkeit," as Fagon calls it (*SW*, 12:124), that reintroduces one to one's own eye and hand, to one's own sensorium. Through painting Mouton and Julian are gradually reacquiring the use of their stunted organs of Edenic consciousness, organs that, in the innocent animal, are already perfectly poised to receive nature. Mouton teaches Julian, who, in contradistinction to his exhausting efforts in the Jesuit academy on the outside, learns readily. Fagon speaks of the boy's "participation in some creative act, production that was effortless and happy, the boldness and independent authority of the shaping hand" (2:82).

The three garden-dwellers represent, then, a kind of hierarchy of Edenic consciousness ranging from the dog through Mouton to Julian. When lost in the stroke of the brush, Mouton and Julian gravitate towards a condition of animal-like innocence in which self as ego ceases to exist, a condition that, while present, makes them completely invulnerable to what Fagon calls the "many checks to . . . self-esteem" (2:82) and, even after its passing, leaves behind enough of its numinous charge to cushion the pain of such checks. But in the full valence of these sublime moments, moments out of time, they shed that lower "self," that onerous cluster of images and ideas generated by language in light of which men generally feel themselves defined, hence seen, hence "imprisoned." Mouton has already come a long way toward the permanent enjoyment of this condition. As a mature painter, he is far more the one who sees than the one who is seen. Indeed, he cares not a whit how he appears to others "with his hat full of holes, . . . in shirt sleeves, and with his baggy stockings," nor does it ever occur to him to bask in the light of the social values promulgated by the Sun King, for he carries on blithely without "the slightest notion of all the grandeur and sublimity your age has produced, Majesty" (2:80–81). It is the dog, however, who is the master, the king, the end-point of this evolution. He is beyond the need of painting or, for that matter, any other form of art or human activity to put him in touch with nature. As "der begabteste," he already *is* nature.

It must be evident by now how strongly Meyer's version of the lapsarian myth echoes the Romantic *Naturphilosophie* of Kleist, Novalis, and even Hoffman, and it will help to shed further light on the quality of life in the Garden—and, ultimately, on the thematic antinomy of consciousness/unconsciousness as a whole—if I bring some of these Romantic echoes into sharper focus.

Perhaps the most elusive issue to be sorted out through a Romantic perspective is that of Julian's intelligence, or supposed lack of it. Most critics agree with the view generally held by the characters in the tale that Julian is, despite his beauty of form and face, irredeemably dull-witted, stupid, or even retarded.[6] This is epitomized in Saint-Simon's dubbing of him as "Le bel idiot" (*SW,* 12:106). But such a judgment means little as an unqualified pronouncement, for one can argue from the perspective of the lapsarian myth that Julian's academic dullness actually signals a far higher, rarer form of intelligence than that displayed by his cultured "betters." In fact, the sort of rote learning over which Julian agonizes at school, designed to inculcate a facile use of language that will enable the student to obfuscate the real world in a nimbus of verbal wit and elegant turns of phrase, that will, in a word, produce a "good courtier," only serves to blight, and eventually destroy, the intuitive gifts that the boy possesses in such abundance. Julian is blessed with an unusually large measure of that intuitive understanding of natural law enjoyed by Adam and Eve before the Fall. It is a pre-verbal sympathy with nature's lively forms and pulsating rhythms. The dog is its perfect fulfillment, a fulfillment to which Mouton and Julian aspire through their Edenic apprenticeships. In the Jesuit academy Julian is again and again seduced from his true education in the real world, that is, in the world of the Garden, through a twisted pseudo-learning rooted in language. But he resists gamely, returning as often as he can to his Academy of Nature. These two schools, the one of the Garden, the other closely affiliated with the court, its head, Tellier, having just been appointed the king's confessor, form an antithesis paralleling that between the two realms whose values they reflect.

What, more precisely, is the nature of the *Bildung* that Julian undergoes in the Garden? Here the older Romantic cosmogony is enlightening. For all his "backwardness" in the Jesuit academy, there are at least three areas in which Julian clearly outshines his fellow pupils: fencing, drawing, and shooting. Excellence in each of these areas requires a high degree of eye-hand coordination. They are rather bodily skills than academic disciplines per se, and Julian is blessed, as Fagon tells us, with "a flawless build that enabled him to excel in every form of physical exercise" (2:75). There is probably no more striking illustration in all of literature of the particular quality of intelligence reflected in fencing than the indomitable bear introduced near the end of Kleist's "Marionettentheater." No man, however skilled, is a match for him, as the author's interlocutor, Herr C., himself a superior fencer, learned to his dismay: "Not just that the bear, like the world's premiere fencer, parried all my thrusts, but he didn't even react to feints (a skill unmatched by any fencer in the world): standing eye to eye, as if able to read my soul therein, paw raised and poised to strike, he would only stir when my thrusts were meant seriously."[7] Herr C. intends the anecdote as an illustration of his notion of "Grazie" (grace), a perfection of corporeal movement that characterizes the inorganic marionette and the naive animal, but is largely denied to self-aware man: "We see that, in proportion as, in the organic world, reflection [i.e., self-consciousness] grows darker and weaker, grace emerges in that world more brilliantly and commandingly."[8] The bear, like Mouton the dog, is at nature's disposal. But man, insofar as he has pridefully placed himself at the center of the universe through the dark powers of self-reference conferred on him by language, can no longer be a perfect instrument of natural law; since he no longer sees the world clearly and directly, but through the symbolizing prism of language experiences himself most often as seen by it, he can no longer act in simple harmony with it. All his movements of body and mind must inevitably be flawed: "Such blunders

. . . have been unavoidable ever since we ate of the tree of knowledge. But Paradise is locked and the cherub behind us."[9]

Julian's "idiocy," his naive manner and his utter estrangement from bookish learning, is the other side of the coin of his special intelligence or *Bildung*—that is, his "Grazie" in Kleist's sense. His academic ineptness is in inverse proportion to his athletic prowess, and necessarily so, since these capacities issue from dynamically antithetical modes of consciousness: "as reflexion grows darker and weaker, grace emerges more brilliantly and commandingly." As awareness dims, be it awareness of self directly or indirectly via scholarly "self-improvement," Eden emerges. In *Das Leiden eines Knaben* academic learning is portrayed as largely a grafting onto the mind of the foreign matter of abstract symbolic systems. (The example given is Julian's futile wrestling with a "foreign" language, Latin, signifying the spiritually alienating nature of language itself—and, by extension, of all symbolic systems derived from it.) Symbols are always one step removed from reality and, as a legacy of man's Fall, are inexorably lured into orbit around that central and most unreal of symbols, the ego, enhancing and embellishing it, confirming its "validity" as a new suit of clothes does the body. By contrast, Julian's true *Bildung* is his education to the simple but elusive grace of seeing and moving. This grace, this intelligence of the body, bestows on him the experience, beyond mediation by any symbol, of his own absorption into nature's dynamic flow. As the effortless unfolding of organic predispositions, Julian's *Bildung* echoes the ideal of education that Goethe and the Romantics derived from Rousseau. It is totally at odds with—indeed, it is undermined by—the force-feeding of conceptual knowledge that passes for education in the Jesuit academy.[10]

Well aware of this, Julian's "mentor" Mouton would spirit the boy away with him to the south of France where he has agreed to do a job for the Marquise de Sévigné. Julian would be his "journeyman" (*Gesellen*) and, there on the lush grounds of the estate, would be able to continue his education for Eden undisturbed, casting off the shackles of a sense-numbing language and giving himself up entirely to the life of the body: "You can come along and stuff yourself with olives. You'll be free as a bird to fly around and snatch up anything you want, wherever you want. You won't have anything more to do with books and compositions" (2:83). As for women, the artificial, blue-eyed Mirabelle would yield to "a nice dark and sun-tanned substitute" (2:84). Mouton's fantasy evokes shades of *Ardinghello* revisited.

Thus the fencing ground, the only oasis of the body available to Julian at the Jesuit academy, becomes by his presence a tiny extension of the Garden into the corrupt society. Ironically, this arena of antagonists, a perverse altar to the relations of power that prevail in the reign of the Sun King, is transformed by Julian into a scene of what can only be called "loving combat." As if by some mysterious power of "Grace," duel evolves into dance and opponents become partners:

> Julian fenced splendidly; I am tempted to say he fenced nobly. During long hours of memory work he had had the mechanical habit of rotating his wrist, and it had become unusually supple. He also had keen eyesight and a very confident attack. He had thus become, as I said, a first-class fencer. He also rode well and intelligently. I assumed that a boy humiliated in everything else would impose whatever superiority he possessed upon his friends to gain their respect. But no, that was beneath him.
>
> Facing him with foil in hand, he treated his skilled opponent and the unskilled one with the same courtesy. Even in the heat of excitement he never wagered with the former or made fun of the latter when he occasionally let them pink him just for encouragement. Thus he demonstrated on the fencing court, gracefully and inconspicuously, the equality that he so painfully existed without during classroom hours.
>
> Among his comrades he enjoyed not the respect gained by his fists, but a shy respect for his inexplicable kindness. . . . The fickleness of fate that embitters so many souls only strengthened and ennobled his. (2 : 84–85)

Fagon's eloquent description of Julian as fencer touches on all the facets of the consciousness/unconsciousness antinomy under discussion here and even hints at the possibility of a resolution to the antinomy through the power of "Grazie" emanating from Julian. Julian always bests his opponent because his concentration, like that of Kleist's bear, is virtually absolute; he is at one with the activity of fencing: "He . . . had keen eyesight and a very confident attack." "Keen eyesight" refers less to the strength of his physical vision than to this power of concentration or absorption in the activity. Julian simply *sees* his opponent. There is no room in his awareness for anything else. The latter, on the other hand, is always partially distracted by the desire to shine, to *be seen* as superior. Julian never fences "to gain . . . respect," but always and only to express spontaneously the joy of graceful movement. His utter indifference to the outcome of the match, even to the extent of occasionally letting his opponent score, is contagious. His opponent soon catches the spirit of the dance, losing awareness of self as he enters that Edenic sphere in which all discrete movements of opposition melt into a single synchronous rhythm. Not knowing quite what to make of it all, a bit embarrassed over being thus strangely, albeit delightfully, "seduced," Julian's opponents come away from the match filled with "not the respect gained by his fists, but a shy respect for his inexplicable kindness." Respect, the grudging tribute one man pays another in a society based on relations of dominance and submission, is elevated to something akin to reverence, the natural expression of wonder in the presence of the sacred.

Less fortunate than Julian's opponents is the fencing master, who deserves mention here since he, too, carries the theme of seenness as unconsciousness and takes his modest place in the picture of a society blinded by delusions of self-reference. Fagon describes him as "an old scarred-up sergeant who had been with the marshall for many years" and who "was deferring to his commanding officer's son, a boy who had been on the schoolbench with other children just a moment ago. His respect was almost subservient, as though he were awaiting an order instead of issuing one" (2:84). The fencing master does not see Julian at all but projects an image of the boy's father, his old commander, onto him and proceeds to behave towards the projection with his long-accustomed obsequiousness, as if the stern superior himself were watching and weighing his every move.

This same ego-less identification with the unerring instincts of his own body, entailing an obliviousness to the whole issue of success or failure, also accounts for Julian's other fortes, shooting and drawing. Like fencing, these skills call for the precise coordination of eye and hand. Seeing versus seenness runs through the entire marksmanship episode, which Julian sadly confides to Fagon, like alternating major and minor chords. Julian and friend Guntram are visiting the latter's uncle, a high-ranking officer, on his estate for "a real test of hand and eye" (2:90). Despite his severe nearsightedness (a physical affliction underscoring his psychological blindness), Guntram is obsessed with the desire to become an officer and will entertain no other career options: "It was the army, of course. He wasn't interested in anything else" (2:90). Thus burdened by an image of himself that can never be realized, Guntram is wider of the mark in the shooting exercise than his poor physical vision alone would account for: "Not a single one of his shots hit. . . . He bit his lip and got terribly worked up. That made his hand unsteady. All the time my shots were hitting the black zone because I could see and aim well" (2:91). The terror with which Guntram lives of not "passing muster," of being seen as unfit, is concentrated here in the image of the uncle whose observing presence causes the nephew's hand to shake uncontrollably. By contrast, Julian, who is aware only of the target, simply sees, aims, fires, and hits.

Even the uncle's departure cannot blot out Guntram's sense of his critical eye, for several draughts of wine fail to still the boy's shooting hand. In despair, he runs off into the brush, bent on turning the pistol on himself and ending it all. He has in mind a suicide pact with Julian, since

"You're no good in life either, even though you do shoot well. You're a big blockhead and the laughing-stock of the whole world!"

"And God?" I asked.

"That's a fine God," he sneered, raising a fist at the heavens above him, "that gave me a love of battle and poor eyes and you a body without my mind!" We struggled, I disarmed him, and he disappeared into the woods. (2:91)

"A body without any mind" is indeed an apt description of Julian, as of Kleist's marionette, "mind" understood as self-consciousness. In terms of the tale's mythical dimension, this is precisely Julian's Grace, by dint of which he is able to be at one with nature. Fagon senses something of this—but again, only something—when he links Julian to the first beatitude according to which "to the poor in spirit belongs the kingdom of heaven" (2:92). But out of the mouth of the bitter Guntram the expression is merely the last in a barrage of insults, and somehow this time, perhaps for the first time, the insults strike a nerve in Julian, marking the beginning of his tragic awakening from the dream-reality of Eden. "From that day on," he laments to Fagon, "I was miserable, for Guntram had put into words what I knew but had concealed from myself as best I could" (2:91). It is at this point that the delicate balance of Julian's spiritual allegiance tilts from Eden to the Fallen society. The concerns of self, so long held in abeyance but finally driven into the center of awareness by relentless social pressure, begin to overshadow the selfless, intuitive enjoyment of nature within and without. What Julian, by virtue of his Grace, had always managed to slough off easily before—the derision of others—now begins to take its toll, and his Fall, in the sense of a fatal reversal of spiritual direction from seeing to seenness, can be said to have commenced. The gates of Paradise are closing behind him and the Cherubim takes up his post before them. But before following Julian out into the fallen world, let us complete our map of Eden, as surveyed from the lofty bluffs of Romanticism, with some further observations on Julian's other talent, drawing, and on his artist-mentor, Mouton.

What I have said of Julian's fencing and shooting applies equally to his facility in drawing. Here, too, any sense of ego, manifesting itself in the desire for a good result, melts into the easy coordination of eye and hand for its own sake. When Julian paints, there is no painter, only painting. In this sense creativity in Julian is very much as the Romantics regarded it, i.e., essentially a rarefied state of consciousness inclusive of any behavior that might issue therefrom, "artistic" or otherwise; whatever product might result from the behavior flowing from this state is a minor matter. This is certainly the sense one gets from Fagon's observations of Julian and Mouton during their leisurely "Malstunden" in the garden. Blissfully ignorant of the "requirements" of form and composition, Mouton paints as the spirit moves him, as it abruptly does, for example, when he is reminded of Père Amiel's prominent nose: "And Mouton, without any suggestion of caricature, sketched a nose with his impudent brush on the easel's pine frame, but what a nose, a monster of a nose, a nose of epic proportions, and so funny that you had to laugh in spite of yourself" (2:82–83). Later Fagon stresses the absence of any conscious effort or deliberate design in Mouton's execution of the prophetic Pentheus drawing, almost as if the drawing had used Mouton as a mere passive vehicle of self-creation: "Mouton himself may not have fully appreciated the evil omen he had conjured up on this piece of paper in an idle moment of creativity" (2 : 90).

The same Romantic emphasis on art as process, as a spontaneous yet controlled movement of consciousness, rather than as project, runs through Fagon's description of Julian and Mouton as they work together on a pastoral painting, a collaboration betokening unawareness of any sense of individual authorship. Again, the quality of effortless inspiration, of a miraculous quickening of the sensorium, predominates, along with the pointed absence of its antithesis, calculating intellect and egoic consciousness with its vulnerability to critical judgment: "Naturally it was mostly Mouton's work. But the boy also had a certain skill with the brush. . . . the participation in some creative act, production that was effortless and happy, the boldness and independent authority of the shaping hand that the unimaginative boy had never before suspected and that he now regarded as a miracle—it clearly made him feel extremely happy after so many checks to his self-esteem. The blood of passion lent color to his pale cheeks, and an enthusiasm he had never known gave wings to his hand. Even I felt a noble surge of paternal happiness" (2 : 82).

It seems best, then, to view Julian's various skills as of one piece, as so many behavioral expressions of a discrete and unified Edenic consciousness in which the subject-object dualism of fallen man is superseded by an identity of actor, activity, and thing acted upon. Thus there is no fencing opponent to be bested, no bull's eye to be hit and no image to be reproduced, but simply a naive state of awareness in which the result is somehow already contained within the act and hence need not be considered.

This disappearance of the "otherness" of the object issuing in natural, effortless creative activity makes of Julian something of a latter-day Romantic artist, particularly of the type fashioned by Hoffmann. Allowing for differences of emphasis, there are several fascinating parallels, for example, between Julian and Anselmus, the hapless hero of *Der goldene Topf*. Both are students floundering in conventional academe who find their true calling in "apprenticeships" to Edenic animal "masters," Archivist Lindhorst being, under the skin, a princely salamander fully cognizant of his pre-human lineage with its roots in the valley of Atlantis. Both undergo a period of artistic training, Julian in painting and Anselmus in poetry, in which art in the material sense is far less important than the condition of cosmic enlightenment it reflects and nurtures. Both are *Sonderlinge*, out of step with and out of place in society, strange ahistorical vestiges of a race long since vanished from earth but to which humanity may ultimately evolve. Both are exponents of the essentially Romantic evolutionary vision, itself a quasi-secular extension of biblical teleology, and, as such, are calculated to make us more aware of our temporal floundering "zwischen Erinnerung und Ahnung."[11] In *Der goldene Topf*, of course, all this is made explicit, while in Meyer's tale it is implicit in the mythical subtext.

When Julian tries to function in society on its own terms, when he enters the sphere of influence of the self-important luminaries at school or court, he is inevitably a bungler, again like Anselmus, who seems unable to greet a Dresden blueblood "without flinging my hat away or even slipping on the slick floor and flopping down disgracefully."[12] Those closest to grace seem to act most gracelessly, to flounder most in its absence, when under the intermittent spell of self-awareness. But when Julian plies his skill on the fencing ground or on the shooting range or at the easel, he moves toward the rarefied sphere of the marionette whose movements, performed in perfect ego-less surrender to a higher power, are infallible. He is in that moment an instrument of *Grazie*, enjoying the full support of natural law.

Meyer, of course, can be assumed to have been as familiar as Kleist with the Christian doctrine of grace as an unearned and, most often, transient state of sanctification, and there seems little doubt that he had something like the idea of sanctifying or purifying grace in mind as a central principle of Julian's characterization. Then again, the *idea* of grace, if not the name, and of the perfect integrity of behavior it empowers, is a cornerstone of most of the world's great religions and has certainly been pondered by any artist, "religious" or not, who has ever felt himself in the throes of creative inspiration. For Hoffmann it is what enables Anselmus to concentrate "attention and thought ever more firmly on the . . . parchment scroll"[13] until the arcane script finally yields its secrets, the loss of which later plunges him into the purgatorial glass bottle. The Christian martyrs relied on it to provide the perfect equanimity with which they endured those appalling tortures. The medieval mystics awaited its epiphany in meditation as a lifeline to the longed-for *unio mystica*. The dervish comes under its sway as he loses himself in his whirling trance. It is what liberates Arjuna, the hero of the *Bhagavadgita*, from the indecision that paralyzes him in the moments before battle. The yogi, when reclining on his bed of nails, may identify it negatively as "detachment," or, when strolling on his carpet of glowing coals, refer to it with understated reverence as "skill in action." For the Zen archer it is what delivers the arrow to the center of the bull's eye with every shot, or, for the Zen swordsman, what reveals his opponent's next thrust a split second before it occurs to the latter to make it. This last example brings us full circle to fencing, Kleist's unerring bear, and, finally, to Julian whose Edenic state of grace makes of him only slightly less glaring an anomaly in human society than his ursine brother would be.[14]

There is one apparent difference between Julian and Anselmus that merits examination, precisely because it *is* only apparent and reveals, under scrutiny, an even deeper affinity between the two. Julian is becoming a painter,

Anselmus a poet (his transcription of Arabic manuscripts a metaphor for the unfolding linguistic-creative process). One is engaged in plastic art, the other in verbal. Whereas *Der goldene Topf* is an apotheosis of poetry, *Das Leiden eines Knaben* contains, as has been seen, a subdued but persistent anti-verbal strain as a thematic corollary of the lapsarian myth: the word tends to corrupt, the word is dangerous. Mouton's wish for Julian, it is recalled, is that "You won't have anything more to do with books and compositions." Hence Julian thrives through painting, a non-verbal form of art that draws him away from the psychological entanglements of language towards an ever increasing capacity for direct visual penetration of reality. (In the single instance in the narrative in which verbal art is highlighted—the early discussion of a performance of Molière's *Le Malade imaginaire*—*Dichtung* comes off rather badly, as I will show later.[15]) It might seem at first blush, then, that Meyer and Hoffmann are somewhat at odds with one another in the aesthetic implications of their themes. But the apparent disparity pales when one realizes that even poetry itself is for Hoffmann merely the objective correlative of a gradually crystallizing cosmic consciousness. The word, even when elevated to the aesthetic dimension—indeed, especially then—is properly an exercise, an exacting medium on which to hone awareness, somewhat like a Zen *koan* whose alogical riddle character is analogous to the inscrutable hieroglyphs that confront Anselmus. Hence the initial tedium of his work as "copyist" and Hoffman's coy disinterest in showing us even a single line of his transcription. The language of poetry is no more than a signpost, a pointer that can be gradually discarded as Anselmus comes closer and closer to a beatific apprehension of nature, which is what all those "strangely intertwined signs, . . . dots, dashes and marks and flourishes"[16] eventually become for him. For both Anselmus and Julian art is the royal road leading back—or forward—to an Eden that has no need of language to mediate understanding.

Mouton knows well that language and the rational intellect have made nature more opaque than transparent to civilized man and that they must now be somehow transcended if he is to regain Paradise. He tries to keep this insight squarely in Julian's awareness, not only through the "de-programming" exercise of painting, but also through the occasional sarcastic observation on language and academic learning, a running commentary of snipes that constitute a kind of inverse or *Un-bildung*. On hearing that Julian has been made to repeat a grade, he snaps, "If you're having trouble with your classwork, then that just proves your healthy normality" (2:83). He doggedly insists on concrete expression and abhors all linguistic abstraction, since the abstract is mere generalization with no extra-mental existence and can only separate man further from nature. A triangle, for example, is no more than "the stupid word" (2:82) and nature itself, if it must have a name, will be called simply "nature" and not the mystifying "creation," since, as

Fagon says, "he could never conceive of the latter, neither in word nor in essence, since he had grown up in depravity and without the catechism" (2:82). (When, in spite of everything, Mouton does resort to abstraction, for instance, "*das Erhabene*" [*SW,* 12:125], it springs from his absorption in a specific physical object: Père Amiel's nose. *Das Erhabene* means nothing if it is cut loose from the tangible things in which it manifests itself.) The very masters of the word, the great poets and dramatists who grace the reign of Louis XIV, mean nothing to him, for "Mouton couldn't read, any more than his pet—the other Mouton—could" (2:81). It bears repeating that Mouton would, were it in his power, whisk Julian off to the balmy south where "You won't have anything more to do with books and compositions."[17]

Mouton's occasional bent for the pithy reflection, usually admonishing against the tendency to reflect, shows him to be more than the noble savage that Reinhardt has labeled him.[18] For all his soft primitivism he is something of a philosopher, an aware savage, as it were. With his rare blend of instinctual genius (his painterly *Grazie*) and a reflective intelligence that, in terms of the myth, has probed as deeply as such intelligence ever has to, that is, to a recognition of the lethal snares of a consciousness grounded in language, he is to be regarded as a highly evolved being whose transcendent vision, even more than his Bohemian exterior, makes him appear a kind of benign freak in the eyes of others. The Edenic myth, of which he is perhaps the most integral part, seems to define him as one of the very few among men who have traveled most of the way around the Kleistian world of consciousness, passing through "an endless awareness," having all but shed the scales of language, and who are now re-approaching Eden to see "if there might not perhaps be another opening somewhere in back."[19] He has come close to realizing that spiritual goal for which Tolstoy longed of experiencing life in its utmost, irreducible simplicity.

On the odd occasion when Mouton finds it worthwhile to talk about nature, he offers a slangy sort of Romantic cosmogony that is reminiscent of Novalis. His celebration of the bull, for example, or of Père Amiel's enormous nose as atavistic vestiges of a bourgeoning primordial nature, a nature still close enough to Eden to glisten with its dew, echoes those legends told to Heinrich von Ofterdingen by the traveling merchants, all of which turn on the idea that "In olden times nature as a whole must have been more alive and intelligent than it is today."[20] How tame, how meek and unobtrusive nature has become since the Fall. In the downward turn of its evolution, "a bull in all his strength and impressive size" has given way as norm to "some scrawny human face" (2:82), and, in general, " 'You can see,' he then went on in all seriousness, 'that nature never stands still. She delights in producing something different now and then. But you don't see such things every day now. The old girl has lost her fire' " (2:83).

The primordial procreative fire of nature is now all but extinguished, as if the very instinct of growth itself were succumbing to the embarrassed self-consciousness of human culture, becoming thus sluggish and slowly sapped of its dynamic *Grazie*. Mouton will paint only those odd corners of creation that still beat with a primal pulse, perhaps intending to demonstrate to nature, in the mirror of his work, what she once was and will be again, using his art to nudge her through her present stage of drowsy refinement. Art accelerates evolution.

In this sense Mouton's pastoral paintings are not mere representations of animals. In fact, as I have said, they are not works of art at all in the sense of conscious inventions limited by concerns of form and composition. They are rather like those Paleolithic cave paintings of bison in southern France (where Mouton would like to work), instinctual expressions of the common life-force shared by both painter and subject. Here indeed is Mouton as noble savage, in the anartistic character of his art. The following description by Thomas Merton of the prehistoric cave painters captures the spirit of Mouton's bovine non-art perfectly and even ties it in with our central theme of Edenic consciousness as a now-lost power of seeing uncluttered by reflection:

> The cave painters were concerned not with composition, not with "beauty," but with the peculiar immediacy of the most direct vision. The bison they paint . . . is a sign, a *gestalt*, a presence of the unique and peculiar life force incarnated in this animal—in terms of Bantu philosophy, its *muntu*. This is anything but an "abstract essence." It is dynamic power, vitality, the self-realization of life in act, something that flashes out in a split second, is seen, yet is not accessible to mere reflection, still less to analysis.
>
> Cave art is a sign of pure seeing, nothing else. . . . it represents an expression of direct awareness of a kind we are no longer capable of conceiving. The cave man's art was before all else a celebration of this awareness and of the *wholeness* of his communion with nature and with life.[21]

Merton goes on to speak of occasional flourishes of an atavistic kind of art that, like Mouton's, evidences "greater fidelity to immemorial modes of vision going back into the prehistoric past." These rare artists "seem to be fighting to preserve an essentially Stone Age view of the world and of society, in which all that man now needs from his inventions was once attained and realized in himself."[22] Mouton's artless art and, in general, his utter indifference to the material and cultural "inventions" of his age would stoke the nostalgia of those neoromantic Marxist critics like Lukács for that vanished childhood of the race before it occurred to man that he must process nature in order to make it work for him.

It is just one of these "processings" of nature, a wheeled vehicle, by which Mouton's dog is killed in the Rue Saint-Honoré, ground up, so to speak, in the wheels of the social juggernaut. Mouton himself dies shortly thereafter, succumbing to a dropsical condition aggravated by a bout of excessive drinking during which he assumes the behavioral patterns of the dog. "I used to watch him . . . ," says Fagon, "sitting in his room. . . . he would yawn like a dog or snap his jaws at flies" (2 : 93). On the surface the painter's death seems a simple case of unmanageable grief over the loss of the animal that has been his life's companion.[23] But again the myth suggests more. It intimates at least a semblance of method in Mouton's canine madness and death. The death of his pet could be said to activate in him a consuming wish to accelerate the end phase of his evolution back to nature, a longing for quick completion of the Kleistian circle of consciousness and ultimate merging beyond death with the elemental life of Eden. The warm glow of alcohol reconciles all differences and, just as with the early narcotic stirrings of awareness in Novalis' *Hymnen an die Nacht*, gives a foretaste of that final reconciliation. The canine behavior, which can only seem a grotesque and pitiful aberration from Fagon's medical vantage point, indicates his shedding of the few remaining trappings of ego, the distillation of consciousness down to the innocent level of the animal. It is all part of Mouton's passing through the mind's final barriers to Eden. Appropriately, he is laid to rest in the Garden alongside his canine "master," both now absorbed back into the elemental spirit that is their origin.

While Mouton can be said to experience through death a liberation of the spirit, Julian undergoes, as of the encounter with Guntram, an agonizing death of the spirit that is, as it were, punctuated by his eventual physical death. The caustic insults of the despairing friend ("You're no good in life either. . . . You're a big blockhead and the laughing-stock of the whole world!") mark the beginning of Julian's Fall from Grace. Not nearly so evolved as Mouton, and hence without his ripeness for Eden, he remains vulnerable to pressures from the outside world, and now, for the first time in his life, he feels deeply the sting of another's critical view of him. It is Julian's first taste of the salt of the beleaguered ego.

At this point a close look at the Byzantine chronology of events in the *Binnenerzählung* proves most interesting. One notes that the Edenic painting interlude discussed above actually occurs some months *after* this fatal moment of shift of Julian's psychic center of gravity from predominantly simple to predominantly egoic consciousness during the outing with Guntram. Grace, it seems, had already begun to recede from Julian's grasp by the time of the particular *Malstunde* recalled by Fagon, so that Julian's blissful absorption in nature via painting in that scene is to be viewed rather as a vestige of what was than a sign of what is. In this way Meyer is indicating that Julian's awakening to the constrictions of self is more an asymmetrical organic process than a discrete event occurring in one "fell swoop." Notwithstanding the Genesis myth, in which Adam and Eve's birth into self-awareness is seen to happen in the twinkling of an eye, most accounts of such fundamental shifts from one perdurable state of consciousness to another show these as evolving gradually over time, in increments built upon jerks, fits, and starts, full of forward leaps and backward falls, until, at some indeterminate moment, the new condition becomes more or less fixed in place—whether for better or worse.[24] Thus the young Adonis in Kleist's "Marionettentheater," of whom the narrator tells us, "only the subtlest eye could detect the first traces of vanity, prompted as these were by the favors of women"[25]; or Hoffmann's Anselmus whose first brief penetrations of Atlantis are followed by relapses into his former condition of doubt and despair.[26] It is recalled that Julian, too, had ominous inklings of what was soon to befall him well before the "observable" moment of transformation triggered by Guntram's insults, "for Guntram had put into words what I knew but had concealed from myself as best I could." Something of the condition to come is sensed before the fact (see Jung's notion of prophetic dreams); conversely, something of the earlier condition clings for a while to the later while the later is crystallizing. Julian's idyllic *Malstunde* with Mouton thus becomes a kind of postlapsarian farewell to Eden, a leave taking of nature in the sense of a final backward glance over the shoulder towards home as one is already taking those first hesitant steps into the foreboding unknown.

That unknown is not long in revealing its harshness. Buckling under the pressure of Guntram's verbal onslaught, Julian's outward-directed vision turns in on itself, contracting and finally splitting into "the seer" and "the one who is seen," the judge and the condemned. One is reminded of August Wilhelm Schlegel's pronouncement in the Vienna lectures on the loss of innocence marking the historical shift from antiquity to the modern Romantic era: "Human nature is, to be sure, simple in its foundation, but all investigations show us that no power in all of nature is simple in such a way as to be incapable of dividing within itself and dispersing in opposite directions."[27] In Julian, ontogeny recapitulates phylogeny. In taking himself as an object, in allowing Guntram's value-laden image of him to gain entrance to the inner sanctum of his awareness and take root there, Julian has begun his rite of passage into the Fallen society. It is a tragic day for Guntram, who makes a gesture towards suicide, but even more so for Julian, for Guntram is already long since a lost cause, while Julian only now becomes one. This day has etched itself indelibly in his memory. He looks back on it as a profound turning point, as an end of innocence and a beginning of pain: "I had one awful day [the day with Guntram], and the others weren't very much better. . . . From that day on I was miserable" (2 : 90–91).

From then on Julian comes more and more to see himself as the "idiot" he is in the eyes of others. He parts company with Kleist's bear and joins that of the young Adonis mentioned above who is condemned by his discovery of the mirror to a life of nagging obsession with his own imperfections. Since

Julian's Fall into seenness occurs well into adolescence, at a time when he is already being held strictly accountable for social and academic achievement, he is effectively denied the grace period of the child during which one develops the indispensable array of psychological strategies, the grab bag of masks and artifices to be displayed to self and others that helps one sustain the burden of ego. He stands stark naked before his own and others' censuring glare. The slings and arrows, thus unbuffered, strike deeper, and Julian rapidly falls into a malaise of self-reference bordering on paranoia: "I kept hearing the word 'blockhead' being whispered behind me, in the street, at school. I pricked up my ears just to hear the awful word. Perhaps, too, the other boys who never bothered me just called me that as a nickname whenever they thought they were out of my hearing. And even Old Lizzy, the woman with the funny wrinkles who sells rolls in front of the school, tries to cheat me. Frequently she's not at all subtle about it, just because she hears them calling me stupid" (2:91).

Since his ears are now primed to hear nothing else, sneering whisperings of his idiocy now assail Julian from all corners. Even his protector Fagon comes under suspicion. When the latter smiles benignly at his simplistic speculations on God, he is appalled at this "tacit mockery" of his stupidity—and, what is worse, he accepts it, since it confirms what he now "knows": "The boy was frightened, by himself and by me" (2:92). Perhaps worst of all, his tortures are not confined to the present; in his fallen state the past, too, is transformed into a house of distorting mirrors as once-neutral memories of social *faux pas* now take on grotesque shapes, revealing to him the full horror of his imagined inadequacy. His botched introduction to the king at Marly, for example, had not pained him deeply at the time; as Maintenon recalls in the frame, he seemed to come away from his defeat "without showing—at least outwardly—any deep signs of the humiliation he felt" (2:70). But now that he is irrevocably self-aware, his memory of the event becomes a source of agony: "Then, as though he had already spoken for too long, he said hastily [to Fagon in their heart-to-heart talk] and not without some bitterness, for his confidence had deserted him again while he had been talking: 'Now everyone knows that I'm stupid, even the king, and he's the one from whom I so wanted to keep it a secret' " (2:92).

Through his Fall Julian becomes a hapless pawn in the power relations that constitute the structure of the "unconscious society," the society of "the seen," and his destruction proceeds apace. He is now more one of them than one apart, yet he is a lamb thrown to the wolves, for he is totally without the character armor that fends off "the watcher" and mediates egoic strivings. Tellier, of course, is the prototypal wolf—Julian experiences him as such ("The wolf [in the zoological garden] reminds me of someone" [2:85])—who lies in ambush, ready to pounce on his prey at the first opportunity in order to avenge himself on his mortal enemy, the boy's father. Through him

Meyer presents a scathing indictment of the militaristic educational system of the Jesuits rivaled in modern literature perhaps only by that of Joyce in his *Portrait of the Artist as a Young Man*.[28] Still it is not the harsh discipline of school that kills Julian, nor even the beating administered, unjustly, by Tellier per se; it is rather the humiliation he suffers that turns a survivable beating into a fatal one. Humiliation, as a form of psychic pain arising from a conviction of one's own worthlessness, is a liability of fallen man; it is a land mine to be found only in the field of self-consciousness. (With its Edenic antipode, humility—a state Julian has now forfeited—the entire matter of self-worth is of no concern.) It is the damage inflicted by Tellier on Julian's fragile—indeed, already pathological—sense of self, not his body, that is critical. Fagon and Argenson recognize this and agree to focus their initial efforts on relief of the boy's mental anguish. A lethal blow to the ego calls for heroic healing measures. Thus Fagon recalls how Argenson urged him to hurry to Versailles:

> "Tell His Majesty everything. He will hold out a hand to Julian and tell him, 'The king respects you; you have suffered too much!' The boy will be as good as unwhipped."
> I agreed with him. This was the best thing to do, the only really helpful thing, if we weren't already too late. (2:101)

But help does come too late, and it is, of all people, Mirabelle who intercepts Fagon's effort to repair the psychological damage done Julian with an offhand pronouncement at dinner that deals him the final blow. Pressed by the prestigious company for an opinion on corporal punishment, she as usual covers herself with the fig leaf of rhetoric: "No subject of the proudest of all kings can tolerate the idea of acts of physical violence; a man so branded will refuse to go on living!" (2:103). The girl whose love is the last remaining mirror of Julian's self-worth shatters that mirror through a reflex act of self-protection that unwittingly confirms his sense of failure as a man. The mirror of identity fashioned from the values of the other—even the benevolent other—carries the same liability as the sword of the Gospel: he who lives by it dies by it.

Julian's beating points up another facet of the tale's anti-verbal theme, for it is nothing other than a mischievous pun devised by a classmate (*"bête à miel* and *bête Amiel"* [2:95]) and falsely attributed to the unsuspecting Julian that provides Tellier with a pretext to pounce. Linguistic dexterity, the clever use of words to conceal even as they reveal, is essential to one's education for life in the fallen society. A fledgling skill in verbal manipulation is evidence that long training in Jesuit casuistry has taken hold in Julian's classmates. This portends future success for them in the nimble, gilt-edged discourse of their parents' aristocratic circles. Julian, on the other hand, is not yet alert even to the pun, this least subtle form of the word's inherent duplicity, and it is his undoing.

The pun, of course, is merely an excuse for Tellier's attack, but even his true motive revolves around linguistic deception, perpetrated in this case by the Jesuits themselves. Contractual agreements written in disappearing ink had enabled the Society to swindle the four brothers out of their land. Aided by Fagon's chemical detection, Marshal Boufflers had uncovered this horrendous sleight of verbal hand, thereby bringing down the Society's covert wrath on himself and his son.

The Society of Jesus is shown to be steeped in linguistic perversion, its inordinate political power and material wealth generated by a fiendishly facile abuse of words. The theft engineered by script "no longer there"; the rhetoric class of Amiel that services as an academic showcase for visitors, featuring the style and form of language at the expense of its substance; the fetishistic cultivation of "logic and dialectics" (2:75) as intrinsic values; the self-ingratiating tones of Tellier as he tells the king of his lowly social provenance ("this despicable talk of his own father, this fawning, hypocritical lying" [2:70], to quote Fagon)—all symptoms of a collective ego's lust for expansion through the word, the instrument of its own creation. And it is the ego, thus elevated to quasi-divine status and enshrined in the Jesuit self-image, that is the real theocracy here, the empire within an empire, the *"Gesellschaft"* within a *Gesellschaft*, the Sun King's France being merely another of the myriad scenes of its historical concretization.

The Jesuit ego is epitomized in Tellier, almost to the point of caricature. At this point, I must briefly recapitulate and expand the analytical concepts I have abstracted from the tale's mythical subtext in order to show how Tellier is included in their purview—and, "on his shoulders" in a later discussion, Fagon and the king. As has been seen, the hallmark of egoic or self-consciousness as delineated in *Das Leiden eines Knaben* is the experience of seenness. Through the symbolizing function of language, one is able to hold an idea or image of the self in the mind. Mistaking this reified idea-image for the dynamic reality it only darkly reflects, one clings to it as to nothing else. In a perverse fulfillment of the serpent's promise, one becomes one's own God. (It would be more precise to designate fallen man's state as one of self-*image*-consciousness rather than self-consciousness; the latter is actually a more appropriate description of the Edenic state in which the illusory God-self or cosmos-self division is absent.) Since the self-image is a "thing" of sorts, an entity of the mind, it is, in a sense, "visible." In being visible, it is felt to be exposed to the judgment of others, premier among whom is that "other" in oneself who holds up the mirror. This vulnerability of what is most precious to judgment from alien sources transforms the world from a place (Eden) one sees (though, strictly speaking, "one" does not exist as such when seeing is occurring) into an omnipotent observing agent by which one is seen (exile). Further, man's fallen state of seenness is emotionally constituted in the tale along a spectrum ranging from pleasure to pain, pride to inferiority. Some of the characters (for instance, Tellier, Julian's father, and, at times, Louis) feed off the pleasure of others' respect and admiration, whether real or fancied, while other characters (such as Mirabelle, Mimeure, and, at different times, Louis) suffer the pain of ridicule, again real or imagined. Common to all characters outside the Garden, however, is the condition of being caught up in seenness; celebrated or snubbed, oppressor or oppressed, each is on the same Ship of Fools, blindly reacting to the experience of an observing presence. The seenness theme, as it unfolds through the strands of myth, stresses this overarching perspective on the entire pleasure-pain spectrum of emotion as the unitary, discrete, continuous field of self-consciousness, what one might call the field of egoic desire. Wherever a character may stand on it, he is to be understood as essentially enmeshed in a half-life of self-reference, a psycho-spiritual limbo, ceaselessly driven by the cravings of ego, unaware of the realm of Edenic freedom lying just outside that ego's encapsulating bubble. Egoic pain is pain, but so too, ultimately, is egoic pleasure, since it is no less a condition of enslavement, no less intrinsic to the Fall. One is condemned to live in fear of losing it, just as the sufferer lives in fear of never having it again.

The underlying fear of loss that nibbles away at self-esteem, like the worm at the core of the apple, erupts into panic when Tellier is informed by Argenson that Julian may be of royal blood and is confronted with the repugnant choice of apologizing to him or possibly forfeiting his appointment as royal confessor. His first impulse is to apologize, but his revulsion over the image of himself thus humbled before the boy quickly overwhelms him, and he absconds. No matter that this *Erniedrigung* would have been kept in strictest confidence; it is enough that he himself would have witnessed it. He will even sacrifice the newly acquired power and status he so covets in order to protect what he covets even more—his self-image as a man above all moral obligation, the source of his own authority. Fagon may not be certain whether "der eine Dämon seines Ordens . . . den andern, der Stolz den Ehrgeiz überwältigt [hatte]" (*SW*, 12:152), but the reader is left with no doubt that Tellier's seenness, in the form of a consuming satanic pride, is his ruling passion. His furious "Was habe ich mit dem Nazarener zu schaffen?" followed by the equally blasphemous slip of the tongue, "Ich bin der Kirche! Nein, des Ordens!" (*SW*, 12:150), and surrounded by mythical associations with Satan ("wie ein Dämon," "der eine Dämon seines Ordens," "diesem Feinde der Menschheit . . . mit seinen Dämonenflügeln" [*SW*, 12:150–53]), points to that first look into the mirror, that first seduction by the ego that impelled Lucifer to covet the throne of God, thereby betraying his own name as the "bearer of light," the light of consciousness.

Since Tellier would be a God unto himself, he finds himself measured by his own godlike standard of diginity, which will brook not even the slightest compromise, far less contrite prostration before a perceived nonentity like Julian.

The Tellier-Julian relationship is fraught with the irony of satanic myth. The Jesuit, the devotee of Jesus, is the Antichrist in disguise, the humble peasant masking the arrogant autocrat, the (sacerdotal) lamb concealing the wolf, over against the true Christlike humility of Julian—or the prelapsarian Julian, to be precise. The irony takes on grotesque hues paralleling those that inform Dostoevsky's darkly obsessive vision of the Second Coming: Tellier is the Grand Inquisitor playing to Julian's unrecognized Christ returned—or even better, to Julian's Prince Myshkin, another redemptive "idiot" crucified on what Dostoevsky elsewhere called, in a metaphor singularly befitting the idea of the conditioned, unconscious society, "the anthill."[29]

One sees, then, that Meyer has invested Julian with features not only of Adam but also of Christ, the Second Adam. Indeed, Julian's characterization is laced with messianic motifs from beginning to end: Fagon's promise to extend to him nothing less than the heroic protection given the Christ child by Saint Christopher: "But if you'll trust in me, I'll carry you through the waves" (2:92); Amiel's protestation of Julian's innocence: "Julian is as innocent as our Savior!" (2:99); Fagon's reference to Julian's beating as "the Golgatha of the Jesuits" (2:104); Tellier's repudiation of both Christ and Julian in the same language, almost in the same breath: "Was habe ich mit dem Nazarener zu schaffen? . . . Und was habe ich mit dem Knaben zu schaffen?" (*SW*, 12:150–51); and Julian's "Last Supper," attended by not one but a host of Judases, celebrated sycophants all, the supreme betrayer, however, none other than the righteous and honorable Marshal Boufflers, who has "sold" his own son in bondage to his enemies.

There is one further messianic motif that requires more extended discussion since it is far subtler than the others and brings together the major themes of language and self-awareness on a general societal level. In recalling the performance of Molière's *Le Malade imaginaire* at which he first laid eyes on Julian's mother, Fagon, at the king's request, recites from memory part of the speech of Doctor Diafoirus in which the deluded father expresses his pride in a son who, in everyone else's eyes, is a hopeless simpleton. Fagon begins his recital with "It is not for the reason that I am his father, . . . but I may perhaps observe that I am entitled to be satisfied with this son of mine" (2:72). The narrator's "surprise" at Fagon's intimate knowledge of the character, "whose role he oddly enough knew by heart" (2:72), immediately alerts one to another of those occasional tongue-in-cheek narrative postures of Meyer's, intended here to direct the reader to Molière's text to check the accuracy of Fagon's memory. In so doing, one finds that he departs just enough and in just the right way from Dr. Diafoirus's dialogue ("ce n'est pas parce que je suis son père, mais je puis dire que j'ai sujet d'être content du lui")[30] to put us in mind of another father's proud pronouncement: "This is my beloved Son, in whom I am well pleased" (Matt. 3:17). This veiled allusion to God the Father's sanctioning of His Son is to be read, I believe, as Meyer's, that is, the artistic "father's," sanctioning of his scorned protagonist, Julian, from an analogous quasi-transcendent (i.e., supratextual) perspective. The Gospel paraphrase links Diafoirus's son Thomas, "a young man without falsehood . . . gentle, peaceable, and on the quiet side" (2:72–73), to Christ, the prototype of these new socially seditious virtues, and, since Thomas is a reflection of Julian in the eyes of his mother, "the troubled woman" (2:73), as she views the play, it links Julian to Christ as well. Through this oblique authorial "underwriting" of Julian's Christlike sanctity, Meyer is in effect rendering invalid the mockingly cynical attitude towards the "soft," taciturn Christian virtues advanced by the drama and uncritically received by the audience (not excluding Fagon).

Moreover, the God's-eye vantage point of the author reveals this cynicism to be symptomatic of a process of unconscious social conditioning in which court dramatist and aristocratic audience mutually reinforce each other. The playgoers are tickled to learn that, as a boy, Thomas Diafoirus "never spoke a word. . . . They had trouble teaching him to read, and even when he was nine he didn't yet know the alphabet" (2:73). Through this shared hilarity over the semi-literacy emblazoned on the features of Thomas's—and by symbolic extension, Julian's—"incredibly dumb face" (2:73), a nexus of values inimical to the true Christian spirit, and implicitly exalting such qualities as wit, articulateness, and intellectual display (what Dr. Diafoirus calls "a very active power of imagination" [2:72]), insinuates itself the more deeply into the consciousness of the ruling class attending the comedy. This consciousness in turn determines the power structure of all institutions of the Fallen society. Meyer is here depicting in miniature the insidiously subtle operation of what Michel Foucault would later call the prevailing *episteme*, the shared ideological framework of a culture within which all experience is interpreted and evaluated, and which anesthetizes all strata of society against the disturbing influence of new points of view.[31] (This "general anesthesia" of the dissenting consciousness is most poignantly demonstrated in Julian's mother who, while loving her son unconditionally, indicates in her "expression of sad disappointment" [2:73] unquestioning submission to the comedy's ideological bias.) What stronger chains are there than the chains of one's own ideas and values, the chains forged by the abstractive powers of language? And if language is, as seems here to be the case, both the forging power and the chain forged, both the instrument and the substance of the ideology promulgated by the theatre event, then it must be a strong chain indeed, for it is exercising something tantamount to a self-sustaining hold over the minds of the playgoers. Should an "alien" being, someone in touch with a reality beyond language, suddenly appear, he will automatically be perceived by those within the episteme's linguistically constructed reality as "the incredibly dumb face" or as "le bel idiot" and thereby nullified.

As one of the numerous cultural institutions that sustain the Sun King's unconscious "anthill," the Versailles theater implies another, especially striking irony, which is probably why Meyer allows it to figure more prominently in the tale than, say, Julian's abortive reception at court, which could have served just as well to illustrate his theme on the collective level. Fagon expresses the general understanding of the sophisticated literati at court when he describes the function of Molière's comic theatre as a kind of educative mirror: "It is a spirit of comedy that holds not only the most exaggerated things, but with malicious pleasure, even the most human things, under such a mocking light that everything begins to grimace" (2 : 72). Indeed, Fagon had been prepared to see his own profession, perhaps even his own person, held up to "salutary" ridicule in Molière's mirror. But there is an intriguing irony that is generated here by two contradictory metaphorical meanings of the mirror idea, for, although a mirror can be a vehicle by which one sees oneself, yet, if one identifies with the reflected image, as in the case of the young Adonis in the "Marionettentheater," it can also become a vehicle through which one experiences oneself as *seen*—by that critical interior observer.

It is this second idea of the mirror that seems to characterize the experience of the theatre audience: even as Molière's play poses in the classical tradition of the comic theater as an arena of self-insight, it is all the while serving precisely opposite ends, for its true aim is to evoke the audience's secretly nervous identification with the love felt by "stupid old Diafoirus" for his "even more stupid son Thomas" (2 : 72) in order thus through ridicule to subvert that love, thereby "purging" the audience of any lingering, "dangerous" susceptibility to the Christlike simplicity embodied in the boy and to the revolution in social equality such simplicity might kindle. The play conducts its subversion by deftly manipulating each viewer's faculty of self-consciousness, aligning his critical interior observer with its own ideological stance, implicitly conveyed through the satire, and setting that observer against the one felt to be observed, the "Dr. Diafoirus" within each viewer, this image of his own guileless self that is "reflected in the mirror." The venerable tradition of catharsis through drama is diabolically stood on its head, for here is a comedy that is inflaming the very passions of fear and pity that its generic counterpart, tragedy, is meant to purge. As Meyer presents it, Molière's theater is indeed a mirror, but a mirror that imprisons the best part of the viewer within its glass, making his suppressed Christlike core the object of his own ridicule, a mirror that imprisons all the more securely for appearing to liberate. Thus the courtiers in attendance leave the theatre believing themselves fortified by art against an enfeebling malady of the heart, while in reality (the reality framed by the author's God's-eye perspective) they have only been plunged more deeply into that fundamentally human malady of self-consciousness, exacerbated in this instance by the historical episteme's fetishization of language.

In this way Molière's dramatic art is shown to be an unconscious promotion of the materials of its own making, the materials of language, and, ultimately, of that circle of self-consciousness, drawn and closed by language, that is the matrix of all epistemes. Outside the circle, beyond the pale of the "anthill," lies the Garden, which, as we have seen, is the locus of an artistic process of a higher order—the sight-empowering act of painting.[32]

The theater episode, then, takes on a nightmarish cast, the grinning mask of comedy shades off into a grimace, as well it must, for the reader is here made witness to the pernicious social conditioning that makes Julian's later "Golgatha" a foregone conclusion. But if we regard Julian as a messianic force, come once again to restore to men a lost vision of Paradise, we have also, in effect, already regarded him as a failed Messiah, reduced in his humiliation to the common lot of their blindness. As Prince Myshkin is driven mad by the spectacle of physical violence that surrounds him, Julian is undone by the spiritual violence indigenous to the self-conscious society. Perhaps no scene better conveys the poignancy of Julian's loss of Christlike status than the one, discussed above, in which he confesses to Fagon his mounting terror of what seems to him the ubiquitous mockery of others and then wistfully invokes the image of the Savior's balancing hand in human affairs:

> "And yet there is a statue of Christ the Redeemer on the wall of the school. He came down to earth to teach justice toward all and gentleness toward the weak."
> He fell silent and seemed to be reflecting. Then he went on. (2:91)

Julian can now do no more than reflect on Christ's goodness; he no longer actually embodies and radiates it. What had heretofore been a palpable reality, an energizing inner presence, has been removed to the shadowy domain of the ideal. What he had once naively *lived*, he can now only consciously long for.

No final grace or eleventh-hour redemption is vouchsafed Julian on his deathbed. He dies as his newly acquired sense of shame has taught him to live, wrapped in a pathetic, isolating cloud of self-reference. Wishing to ease his son's last moments, the marshal takes advantage of his delirium to suggest to him a battle scenario in which he can play a hero's part: " 'The English flag there! Seize it!' his father commanded. The dying boy reached out. 'Vive le roi!' he exclaimed. Then he sank back as though struck by a bullet" (2:104). This last best hope of the society for spiritual regeneration dies a failed

Messiah. Julian draws his final breath clinging to a delusion of restored self-esteem, hoarding the very psychological currency of Fallen man his special grace once promised to abolish. Intuitively Fagon senses this larger spiritual dimension of Julian's tragedy. He knows that there is more to his death than a megalomaniac's aberrant act of brutality, that, on the most fundamental level, Julian's death represents the society's compulsive seduction and murder of innocence. This is unmistakably reflected in his quick retort to the king's perfunctory expression of sympathy, a cynical affection of good cheer over the last-minute patchwork on Julian's ego—his Fallen self—that closes the tale in a breath of ice: " 'Why poor?' Fagon asked brightly. 'Didn't he die like a hero?' " (2 : 104).[33]

This brings us to the matter of the *Rahmen* and to a final consideration of the two characters, Fagon and Louis XIV, whose deepest significance lies precisely in their relationship as presented therein. Recent critics such as Jacobson and Swales have rightly pointed out that the frame of *Das Leiden eines Knaben* is far more than an elegant window dressing or outer garment for the *Binnenerzählung*. Indeed, it is in the frame where the entire dramatic conflict and suspense of outcome are located, the denouement of the inner story being known from the outset. Julian's already sealed fate becomes the catalyst for a "full-blooded battle of wills,"[34] an electrically charged dialogue between king and physician that "subsumes the interior tale as both an extended argument within the dialog and as a part of the subject matter of the dialog":[35] Will Fagon be able to convince Louis of Tellier's treachery and thereby move him to exact justice and, beyond that, to initiate wider social reform?

I would like to suggest that there is another conflict going on within the frame right alongside, or rather behind, the one between Fagon and Louis, a conflict within Fagon himself that lends depth and texture to the manifest battle of wills and extends the basic theme of seenness into the frame dimension. On the most visible level Fagon seeks to open the king's eyes. He is driven by the need to bring the full brunt of royal outrage down on the murderer of his ward. Less visible, but equally powerful, is another need of Fagon's; it, too, is a need that, it would seem, only the king can satisfy: the need to be forgiven for Julian's death, to be relieved of the crushing burden of guilt over a tragedy he might have prevented. Had he only been more alert, more cautious, more courageous and decisive at the critical juncture, had he only taken Mimeure's warning about the Jesuits to heart: "Mark my words, Fagon, . . . if you don't get him [Julian] released from the Jesuits and provide him with a proper life, . . . by all that's holy" (2 : 88). These and a thousand other daggers of remorse must be seen as constituting a motive for telling his tale to Louis at least as compelling as his desire for retribution against Tellier. If so, then Fagon's tale becomes as much an act of confession as an effort to enlighten,[36] and these two motives can only be seen as working at cross purposes. Fagon's need to confess to and obtain pardon from a higher authority places him in a condition of psychological dependency vis-à-vis Louis, whom he makes into the Royal Father Confessor, the conscience of the realm as it were. This can only undermine the persuasive power so essential to his effort to pierce the thickness of that "shroud" which the king would prefer to leave draped over "unfortunate matters" (2:80). There is no weaker base than guilt from which to attempt to influence others. Such attempts at influence become all the more impotent when one has surrendered one's moral autonomy to the person to be influenced. If Fagon's tale is, in effect, an act of semiconscious or even unconscious self-prostration before the monarch, it is small wonder that the latter can listen to it without being deeply moved, for, notwithstanding his occasional angry outbursts over Louis' willful blindness, the righteous indignation that should be turning his words into hammer blows is being muted by psychological self-interest. Fagon is like a horse whose rider spurs him on while keeping the reins held tightly back.

There are several salient details of Fagon's narrative behavior that point to his obsessive preoccupation with his own guilt and thus imply a confessional motive to his story and a covert seeking of absolution from Louis. Most obvious is his protracted lingering over the bath interlude preceding the ride to Versailles, the recounting of a quarter hour of sustained self-condemnation set against the ironically contrasting background of trivial lamentation issuing from the lovelorn girls in the adjacent stall: "While the water restored my vital energies, I reproached myself sharply for having neglected the boy who had been entrusted to me and for having put off his 'liberation' for so long. . . . There I was, berating my own negligence and dragging around a hundred-pound weight on my conscience, while next to me two silly water nymphs were teasing and splashing each other" (2:101–2). (An added irony here is Fagon's unawareness of the exculpatory motive for his bath, an unconscious attempt to wash away the stain of failure.) Since the entire bath episode revolves around Fagon's own emotional plight and is at best incidental to his immediate narrative concern, which is Julian's fate, it can only be understood as an intrusion of psychological self-interest which he uses to reveal his guilt and fish for royal pardon.

Then there is the agonizing sense of failure that must afflict Fagon for having betrayed his self-appointed role as Saint Christopher to Julian's Christ child. He recalls that he had promised the lad: "But if you'll trust in me, I'll carry you through the waves." Fagon's shame must exist on the same outsized mythic scale as his self-image of Heroic Protector. And when he searches the king's face in vain for some slight hint of outrage over "the proferred unmasking of his confessor" (2:101), might he not be searching for a forgiving look or gesture for himself as well? The self-serving account of the remorse-ridden bath interlude that immediately follows would suggest that he is.

Thus Fagon's righteous denunciation of Tellier is, as it were, tainted by a personal confessional motive that finally renders it impotent. Nor could it do otherwise, for confession is the ultimate form of seenness, the most radical surrender of one's own power of vision to the other, who is thereby made omnipotent. To confess one's sins is not merely to suffer moral self-definition at the hands of the other, but actively to invite it. Subjectively one feels one's very being to have been placed in the other's hands like a piece of clay to be molded as he sees fit. Secretly the penitent can only hate the confessor, resenting bitterly the latter's putative moral superiority and his own abject dependency.[37] The covert penitent-confessor relationship be-tween Fagon and Louis serves to illustrate the ultimate inability of Fallen man to help himself or anyone else. Human society, structured as it is by the principle of seenness, can never be more than an aggregate of victims. How total its discontinuity with the luminous, self-oblivious vision of the Garden community.

Even those who ostensibly rule must be seen as victims in this sense. The great Sun King himself is far less a source of power than a target of the power wielded by the bugaboos of his own imagination, which are principally two: posterity, with its sovereign historical judgment, and the Jesuit order. These are the phantoms of mind by which Louis feels himself watched, under whose sensed scrutiny he enacts his reign and lives his private life. Of the former he says hopefully, "History itself also wields its pen and will judge me and my person within the confines of my time and with understanding" (2:71). But it is the latter, the Jesuits, to whom Louis is most deeply in bondage, for they control his conscience, the conscience of an aging mon-arch who is now less concerned with this world's judgment than with that of the next. Meyer makes it clear at the outset that the Society's control over the king's mind is to be understood as virtually total since the roots of that control lie deep in his unconscious. As the narrator puts it, "He [Louis also believed, incredible as it sounds, for fears that were vague but just wouldn't go away, that he was not permitted to select his confessor from another order" (2:68). The obvious situational irony is that Fagon's appeal to Louis against Tellier is doomed from the start, for the king, though nominally sovereign, has relinquished his personal power to his new Father Confessor, the very man whom Fagon is accusing. Louis is not about to have his eyes opened regarding a man who has become, in effect, the personification of his own conscience.

One sees from this that the suspense of outcome supposedly generated by the frame situation is only apparent. The blindness of self-absorption that afflicts both king and physician amounts to a guarantee of Tellier's invulnerability. Although Fagon is not totally blind, although he has, in mythic terms, access to the Garden and could conceivably become a force for enlightenment, in the end he, too, is neutralized by the miasma of his own guilt and a need for forgiveness that obscures all else. So he "confesses" to Louis who, in turn, stands in a confessional relationship to the satanic Tellier. Indeed, the inner shape of the frame is just this serial structure of confessional relationships. The frame essentially functions, then, as a further expression of the theme of seenness (here in its radical form of confession), the post-Edenic *conditio humana;* it stands as a kind of contrapuntal echo of the lapsarian myth that runs through the interior story.

Nor is it only in the frame's inner shape that one catches this echo; it also resonates through the relationship therein developed between Louis and Tellier, considered in its mythic dimension. Tellier is a satanic figure into whose clutches the king has fallen. He is the arch "enemy of mankind who could, with his demon's wings, cast a shadow over the end of a glorious reign" (2:101). For his part, the king is the prototype of the race; he is Everyman, languishing in the death-grip of Satan, the mythical embodiment of an unregenerate *amour-propre.* The devil's grip is neither more nor less than the grip of seenness, the grip of willful self-absorption that has driven man out of the Garden of Paradise into a garden of quite another kind, a stifling, solipsistic maze, "whose various . . . pathways . . . all came together at one and the same central spot: the king, again and again, the king" (2:101). Fallen man is indeed king over all he surveys, but his perverted vision surveys only the dreary projections of his own paltry ego. The Garden has become a maze, the kingdom of heaven a house of mirrors.

In *Das Leiden eines Knaben* it is not merely this or that individual, or group, or even a particular historical era, but the world itself that has, mythically, gone to the devil, making this quite possibly the most pessimistic of all Meyer's tales. Meyer embeds his characters in a pre- and postlapsarian mythical subtext, but that subtext stops short of any distinct outline of the redemption that resolves and completes the Christian vision. *Das Leiden eines Knaben* holds out only the faintest redemptive hope for man; indeed, through the corruption and murder of the messianic Julian, the very possibility of human redemption is at once tested and found to be unimaginably distant. Odd individuals here and there like Mouton may realize oneness with nature, but the race in general gropes in the darkness of alienated self-absorption. In terms of Romantic teleology, *Das Leiden eines Knaben* performs only the first two steps of the cosmic dance, that of *Präexistenz* and that of exile within history, while maintaining a sober antipathy towards the third step of millennial perfection. In terms of Christian *Heilsgeschichte*, the tale traces only the first or descending half of what Northrop Frye has described as the fundamental U-shape of the Bible,[38] the half encompassing

Eden and the Fall, conspicuously omitting the second, rising half of redemptive optimism.

Steeped as it is in a contemporary absence-of-God anxiety, *Das Leiden eines Knaben* becomes something of a grim meditation on the nature of the coercive power that has constituted man's tortured human relationships since the Fall. Who or what truly wields the power by which one man seems bound to another—for instance, Mimeure to Louis or Louis to the Jesuits? What is the ultimate source of this power? To conclude that the source of power is the one to whom a given individual sumbits misses the mark, because, as has been seen, the king is completely unaware of the psychologically inferior positions of, say, Mimeure and Fagon with respect to himself. One cannot wield power one is unaware of having. On the other hand, to locate power willy-nilly in those who occupy nominal seats of power, in those who rule, resolves nothing because, again as has been seen, the Sun King is, in the final analysis, impotent, a puppet jumping now to Jesuitical strings, now to those of historical judgment.[39]

The lapsarian-mythical dimension of *Das Leiden eines Knaben* suggests that one conceive of that power by which human relationships are structured as a form of perverted grace, specifically as Edenic grace-gone-sour, and that the ultimate source of power is nothing other than man's own satanic sense of seenness by "the other," whether real or, as in most instances, projectively imagined. Man's primal power is his self-oblivious vision, his direct Edenic sight, which he has tragically turned in on himself in the bifurcating act of self-awareness. The awareness, mediated by language, of self as a being distinct from the rest of creation, one's own fundamental sense of individuality, implicitly posits an "other" by whom one is seen. Thus do the exit gates of the Garden swing open as man takes one foot out of nature. The essence of nature's antipode, society, is just this oppressive sense of "the other" by whom one feels oneself seen. Society is simply man's fallen state of self-awareness, or conversely, his loss of awareness of Edenic oneness. Through the suggestive resonance of Christian and Romantic myth, *Das Leiden eines Knaben* arrives at an intuitive understanding of society as the quintessentially human state of unconsciousness; through its radical critique of language as the implement of this unconsciousness, Meyer's tale anticipates such artistic-intellectual developments as the *Sprachkrise* of fin de siècle Vienna and the contemporary structuralist questioning of the capacity of language to mirror anything beyond itself.

Notes

INTRODUCTION

1. My translation from Conrad Ferdinand Meyer, *Briefe Conrad Ferdinand Meyers nebst seinen Rezensionen und Aufsätzen*, ed. Adolf Frey (Leipzig: H. Haessel, 1908), 1:65. Throughout the text of this study, foreign-language sources, both primary and secondary, are almost always quoted in English translation. These translations are my own, unless otherwise acknowledged. The original foreign language is quoted only when it is indispensable to establishing a point of scholarship or interpretation. In the notes, however, foreign-language sources are quoted in the original.

2. Among the pro-fatalists may be numbered: Louis Wiesmann, "Nachwort," *Das Leiden eines Knaben*, by C. F. Meyer (Stuttgart: Reclam, 1966), pp. 68–69; Fritz Martini, *Deutsche Literatur im bürgerlichen Realismus, 1848–1898*, 3d ed. (Stuttgart: Metzler, 1974), p. 836; Arthur Burkhard and Henry H. Stevens, "Conrad Ferdinand Meyer Reveals Himself: A Critical Examination of 'Gustav Adolfs Page,'" *Germanic Review* 15 (1940): 211; Harry Maync, *Conrad Ferdinand Meyer und sein Werk* (Frauenfeld, 1925; reprint, New York: AMS, 1969), p. 222; and Ernst Feise, "Fatalismus als Grundzug von Conrad Ferdinand Meyers Werken," *Euphorion* 17 (1910): 111–43. Feise's article is reprinted in *Xenion* (Baltimore: Johns Hopkins University Press, 1950).
Those who take issue with the above include George W. Reinhardt, "Two Romance Word-plays in C. F. Meyer's *Novellen*," *Germanic Review* 46 (1971): 47–49, and Michael Shaw, "C. F. Meyer's Resolute Heroes: A Study of Becket, Astorre and Pescara," *Deutsche Vierteljahrschrift* 40 (1966): 381.

3. See previous note. In a more recent article, Reinhardt reiterates and elaborates his adamantly voluntarist stance, but here with far greater sensitivity to the other side of the coin and with an intuitive inkling of the ultimate resistance of the issue to logical-intellectual solution. See George W. Reinhardt, "On G. Lukacs' Critique of C. F. Meyer: How Is History Made?" *Colloquia Germanica* 15 (1982): 287–304.

4. Burkhard and Stevens, "Meyer Reveals Himself," pp. 210–11. For a recent recurrence of the stereotype, see Christine Merian-Genast, *Die Gestalt des Künstlers im Werk Conrad Ferdinand Meyers*, Europäische Hochschulschriften: Deutsche Literatur und Germanistik, series 1, 74 (Bern: Herbert Lang, 1973), p. 14, who calls Meyer's art a pale "Ersatz für ein ungelebtes Leben."

5. Two opposite religious types, discussed by William James in his classic *Varieties of Religious Experience* (New York: Mentor, 1958), pp. 76–139.

CHAPTER 1. HISTORICAL CONSCIOUSNESS VERSUS ACTION IN *DAS AMULETT*

1. For a sampling of the first reviews, see the "Anhang" to Adolf Frey's biography, *Conrad Ferdinand Meyer: Sein Leben und seine Werke*, 2d ed. (Stuttgart: Cotta, 1909), pp. 387–90.

2. G[unter] H. Hertling, "Religiosität ohne Vorurteil: Zum Wendepunkt in C. F. Meyers 'Das Amulett,'" *Zeitschrift für deutsche Philologie* 90 (1971): 526–45, and Paul Schimmelpfennig, "C. F. Meyer's Religion of the Heart: A Reevaluation of *Das Amulett*," *Germanic Review* 47 (1972): 181–202, present excellent summaries of the novella's long critical nadir that persisted into the 1970s with Karl Fehr's assertion of "Anfangs-Schwächen" in his book, *Conrad Ferdinand Meyer* (Stuttgart: Metzler, 1971), p. 48.

3. These include John C. Blankenagel, "Conrad Ferdinand Meyer: *Das Amulett*," *Journal of English and Germanic Philology* 33 (1934): 270–79; Helene von Lerber, *Conrad Ferdinand Meyer: Der Mensch in der Spannung* (Basel: Reinhardt, 1949), pp. 314–17; James M. Clark, "Introduction," to *Das Amulett*, ed. James M. Clark (London: T. Nelson, 1955), pp. i–xxii; Louis Wiesmann, *Conrad Ferdinand Meyer: Der Dichter des Todes und der Maske*, Baseler Studien zur deutschen Sprache und Literatur 19, ed. Friedrich Ranke and Walter Muschg (Bern: Francke, 1958), pp. 42, 185; Ipke Nommensen, *Erläuterungen zu Conrad Ferdinand Meyers Das Amulett*, 7th ed., rev., Erläuterungen zu den Klassikern 273 (Hollfeld/Obfr.: C. Bange, 1958); and Keith Leopold, "Meyer and Mérimée: A Study of Conrad Ferinand Meyer's *Das Amulett* and its Relationship to Prosper Mérimée's *Chronique du règne de Charles IX*," *University of Queensland Papers* 1 (1960): 1–13.

4. The novella's present prestige is largely the result of efforts by D. A. Jackson, "Recent Meyer Criticism: New Avenues or Cul-de-sac?", *Revue des Langues Vivantes* 34 (1968): 620–36, and "Schadau, the Satirized Narrator, in C. F. Meyer's *Das Amulett*," *Trivium* 7 (1972): 61–69; Hans-Dieter Brückner, *Heldengestaltung im Prosawerk Conrad Ferdinand Meyers*, Europäische Hochschulschriften: Deutsche Literatur und Germanistik, series 1, 38 (Bern: Herbert Lang, 1970), pp. 22–23, 44–47; Hertling, "Religiosität," and *Conrad Ferdinand Meyers Epik: Traumbeseelung, Traumbesinnung and Traumbesitz* (Bern: Francke, 1973), pp. 73–82, which restates the interpretation given in the earlier article; Schimmelpfennig, "C. F. Meyer's Religion of the Heart"; George W. Reinhardt, "The Political Views of the Young Conrad Ferdinand Meyer with a Note on *Das Amulett*," *German Quarterly* 45 (1972): 270–94; Walter Huber, *Stufen dichterischer Selbstdarstellung in C. F. Meyers Amulett und* Jürg Jenatsch, Europäische Hochschulschriften: Deutsche Sprache und Literatur, series 1, 340 (Las Vegas: Peter Lang, 1979); and Tamara S. Evans, *Formen der Ironie in Conrad Ferdinand Meyers Novellen* (Bern: Francke, 1980), pp. 17–31.

5. Jackson, "Recent Meyer Criticism," p. 633.

6. Jackson, "Schadau, the Satirized Narrator," p. 68.

7. Hertling, "Religiosität," 529; similarly in his book, *Conrad Ferdinand Meyers Epik*, pp. 81–82.

8. Schimmelpfennig, "C. F. Meyer's Religion of the Heart," p. 190.

9. Reinhardt, "Political Views," p. 283.

10. Conrad Ferdinand Meyer, *The Complete Narrative Prose of Conrad Ferdinand Meyer*, trans. George F. Folkers, David B. Dickens, and Marion W. Sonnenfeld (Lewisburg: Bucknell University Press, 1976), 1:67. Subsequent parenthetical volume and page references are to this edition.

11. Jackson places no importance on this scene and does not trouble himself to identify the nature of Schadau's experience. He is content with the generalized statement that "he [Schadau] glimpses the folly of man murdering man because of disagreements about the right way to salvation" ("Schadau, the Satirized Narrator," p. 69). Hertling characterizes Schadau's experience variously as "Traumbild," "Fiebertraum" and "Vision," which, nevertheless, somehow remains an "in sich selbst realistisches Erlebnis" that is "wirklichkeitsnah. . . . Nymphe und Steinfrau sind für ihn keine Märchengestalten, denn er erlebt sie empirisch: er sieht und hört sie" ("Religiosität," p. 535). With less confusion but ultimately no more enlightenment, Schimmelpfennig refers to the experience as a "dream" and as "a religious epiphany" ("C. F. Meyer's Religion of the Heart," pp. 190, 194). Reinhardt, like Jackson, makes no attempt to identify the nature or quality of Schadau's experience, simply remarking that "The goddess of the Seine rises from the bloodstained river to converse with her 'sister,' one of the caryatids of the Louvre" ("Political Views," p. 283). For Evans, the event is simply a "Traum", albeit one of metaphysical import. (*Formen der Ironie*, p. 28). See note 23 below.

12. Robert Crookall, *The Study and Practice of Astral Projection* (1960; reprint, Secaucus, N.J.: Citadel, 1976), p. 1. My references to typical characteristics of the OOBE rely mainly on

Crookall's study. Readers interested in the results of laboratory experimentation with this phenomenon are referred to Charles T. Tart's chapter, "Out-of-the-body Experiences," in *Psychic Exploration*, ed. E. Mitchell and J. White (New York: Putnam, 1974), pp. 349–74, and to Tart's book, *States of Consciousness* (New York: E. P. Dutton, 1975), p. 285.

13. Tart, *States*, p. 285.

14. Crookall, *Study and Practice*, pp. 1, 28, 177.

15. Ibid., p. 19.

16. See reference to Hertling in note 11.

17. Cf., for example, Crookall, *Study and Practice*, p. 185.

18. Jackson, "Schadau, the Satirized Narrator," p. 68; Hertling, "Religiosität," pp. 535–36; Schimmelpfennig, "C. F. Meyer's Religion of the Heart," p. 190; and Reinhardt, *Political Views*, p. 283.

19. The river goddess' slang is a vital aspect of her symbolic function as historical gadfly. This becomes clear when one considers how rarely Meyer allows even his mortal characters, much less a goddess, to speak in less than declamatory, heroic style without a compelling reason. As Arthur Burkhard has observed, "He [Meyer] . . . avoids colloquial words, common foreign terms, and the dialect expressions of provincial speech." See *Conrad Ferdinand Meyer: The Style and the Man* (Cambridge: Harvard University Press, 1932), p. 29.

20. Hertling, "Religiosität," pp. 535–36, in support of his argument that she speaks "von oben," i.e., from a transcendent perspective.

21. Gustaaf van Cromphout, "Emerson and the Dialectics of History," *PMLA* 91 (1976): 54, 64, provides a good summary discussion of the issue.

22. Jackson, "Schadau, the Satirized Narrator," p. 68.

23. Hertling's contention, in "Religiosität," p. 529, that Schadau's vision transforms him from doctrinaire Calvinist into liberal Christian is contradictory, inasmuch as this "conversion experience" supposedly takes place without Schadau's awareness: "Vielmehr möchten wir zeigen, . . . daß der Dichter gerade die innere, wenn auch seinem Helden Schadau selber nicht bewußte Gesinnungswandlung gestaltet: Es ist die Wandlung eines orthodoxen Protestanten zum toleranten Menschen, dem die Gnade Gottes teilhaftig wird." It is hard to conceive of a conversion experience that leaves the conscious mind unaffected. My argument is precisely that Schadau's moment of enlightenment, his "Gesinnungswandlung," is tragically fleeting, limited as it is to the brief duration of his OOBE, and, in subsequently becoming partially lost to memory, leads to no substantial change of character. Evans, like Hertling, regards Schadau's experience as transformative (though she avoids Hertling's logical error): for her it is a milestone in his *Bildung* and signals the humanizing influence on his character of association with such magnanimous spirits as Boccard, Chatillon and Montaigne (*Formen der Ironie*, p. 28). On this critical point I disagree with Evans as with Hertling, and on similar grounds, while at the same time endorsing her larger observation that "Die Worte der Karyatide in der Bartholomäusnacht bilden die weltanschauliche Kernaussage der Novelle: . . . sie morden sich, weil sie nicht einig sind über den richtigen Weg zur Seligkeit" (p. 18).

24. See Maync, *C. F. Meyer und sein Werk*, p. 223.

25. Quoted and translated by Isaiah Berlin, *The Hedgehog and the Fox: An Essay on Tolstoy's View of History* (New York: Touchstone, 1953), p. 18.

26. Brückner, *Heldengestaltung*, p. 46.

27. See Jackson, "Schadau, the Satirized Narrator," pp. 62–63; Schimmelpfennig, "C. F. Meyer's Religion of the Heart," p. 195; and Leopold, "Meyer and Mérimée," p. 8.

28. See Meyer, *Briefe*, 1:32; also Conrad Ferdinand Meyer, *Novellen* 1, vol. 11 of *Sämtliche Werke. Historisch-kritische Ausgabe*, ed. Hans Zeller and Alfred Zäch (Bern: Benteli, 1959), p. 227. Subsequent parenthetical references to this edition in the text will be designated by *SW*.

29. Leopold von Ranke, *Über die Epochen der neueren Geschichte. Vorträge dem Könige Maxmilian II. von Bayern im Herbst 1854 zu Berchtesgaden gehalten*, in *German Literature since Goethe*, ed. Ernst Feise and Harry Steinhauer (Boston: Houghton Mifflin, 1958), 1:163.

30. Quoted by Richard Brinkmann, "Zum Begriff des Realismus für die erzählende Dichtung des neunzehnten Jahrhunderts," in *Begriffsbestimmung des literarischen Realismus*, Wege der Forschung 212, ed. Richard Brinkmann (Darmstadt: Wissenschaftliche Buchgesellschaft, 1969), p. 226.

31. Fehr, *Conrad Ferdinand Meyer*, 49, see also Schimmelpfennig, "C. F. Meyer's Religion of

the Heart," p. 196, for a discussion of Meyer's claims to authorial impartiality in letters to Hermann Haessel (26 May 1873) and Franz Brümmer (11 March 1874).

32. Meyer, *Briefe*, 1:65.

33. In Heinrich Henel, *The Poetry of Conrad Ferdinand Meyer* (Madison, Wisconsin: University of Wisconsin Press, 1954), p. 68.

34. Ibid.

35. Quoted by Margaret R. B. Shaw, "Introduction" to *Scarlet and Black*, by Stendhal (Baltimore: Penguin, 1969), p. 11.

36. In a letter quoted by Wiesmann, Meyer says of himself: "Ich habe . . . Gottvertrauen, so viel ein Kind des neunzehnten Jahrunderts haben kann" (*Conrad Ferdinand Meyer: Der Dichter des Todes und der Maske*, p. 43).

37. Meyer's acquaintance with Platonic thought is documented in Frey's biography (*Leben und Werke*, p. 97). Although there is no reference to Swedenborg in either the letters or Frey's biography, it is inconceivable that Meyer had no knowledge of this most influential of Swedish thinkers, particularly when one considers Meyer's studies of Swedish affairs preparatory to writing *Gustav Adolfs Page* (*SW*, 11:279–86) and the prominence of Swedenborgian societies in Switzerland well into our own century. As for *Faust*, a perusal of the *Briefe*, for instance, 2:206–07, shows that Meyer knew the drama well enough to cite textual differences between the prose *Urfaust* of 1775 and the final version in verse.

38. See "Vermischte Aufsätze," in Meyer, *Briefe*, 2:473–74.

39. Meyer, *Briefe*, 2:272. For an account of Meyer's dabbling in mysticism at Préfargier, see also Lena F. Dahme, *Women in the Life and Art of Conrad Ferdinand Meyer* (1936; reprint, New York: AMS Press, 1966), pp. 41–42.

40. Henel, *The Poetry*, p. 30.

41. Frey, *Leben und Werke*, pp. 144–45, and Fehr, *Conrad Ferdinand Meyer*, p. 35.

42. Schimmelpfennig points out Meyer's paraphrase of a verse from Paul's letter to the Romans: When Schadau, in reflecting on his mixed feelings about Boccard's death, says, "meine Gedanken verklagten und entschuldigten sich unter einander," he is paraphrasing Paul, who says of the heathens with their innate sense of conscience "daß sie beweisen, des Gesetzes Werk sei beschrieben in ihren *Herzen*, sintemal ihr Gewissen sie bezeugt, dazu auch die *Gedanken, die sich unter einander verklagen oder entschuldigen . . .*" (Rom. 2:14–15, italics Schimmelpfennig's; "C. F. Meyer's Religion of the Heart," pp. 193–94).

43. Fritz Martini, "Wilhelm Raabes 'Prinzessin Fisch': Wirklichkeit und Dichtung im erzählenden Realismus des 19. Jahrhunderts," in *Begriffsbestimmung des literarischen Realismus*, p. 304.

44. Brinkmann, "Zum Begriff des Realismus," p. 227. For a fuller discussion of Brinkmann's position, see his book, *Wirklichkeit und Illusion: Studien über Gehalt und Grenzen des Begriffs Realismus für die erzählende Dichtung des neunzehnten Jahrhunderts* (Tübingen: Niemeyer, 1957), especially the last chapter.

45. See note 36.

46. This part of my study is a slightly emended and updated version of my article, "Historical Consciousness versus Action in C. F. Meyer's *Das Amulett*," originally appearing in *Symposium* 32 (1978): 114–32.

CHAPTER 2. *GUSTAV ADOLFS PAGE* AS A TRAGEDY OF THE UNCONSCIOUS

1. In a letter of 25 September 1881, in Anton Bettelheim, ed., *Louise von François und Conrad Ferdinand Meyer: Ein Briefwechsel*, 2d ed. (Berlin: VWV, 1920), p. 23.

2. Von François's letter is dated 16 October 1881. See Bettelheim, *François und Meyer: Briefwechsel*, p. 25. Emil Ermatinger offers persuasive evidence that Meyer derived the idea of a female page from Heinrich Laube's early drama, *Gustav Adolf* ("Eine Quelle zu C. F. Meyers Novelle 'Gustav Adolfs Page,'" *Das literarische Echo* 19 [1916]: 22–26). If von François was likewise familiar with this youthful effort of Laube's, which, although remaining unpublished in the nineteenth century, had been described by the author in detail in his introduction to an 1845 edition of the play *Monaldeschi*, then her guessing of Meyer's "secret" becomes less telepathic.

3. For an elaboration of this point of view, see Karen Horney, *Feminine Psychology*, ed.

Harold Kelman, trans. Edward R. Clemmens, John M. Meth, Edward Schattner, and Gerda F. Willner (New York: Norton, 1973), pp. 80–81.

4. Even Friedrich Kittler, who brings to the tale many insights of Freudian and Lacanian psychoanalysis, nevertheless does not distinguish between conscious and unconscious narrative levels as such; rather he views the tale within a combined framework of discourse and speech-act theory in terms of the opposition between valid and invalid discourse, or, more precisely, between discourse and its absence, the latter exemplified by such phenomena as dreams (for example, Gustel's *Wunschtraum* of serving under the king) in which "communication" is unilateral, private or interior, there being no real "Hörer" (*Der Traum und die Rede: Eine Analyse der Kommunikationssituation Conrad Ferdinand Meyers* [Bern: Francke, 1977], pp. 7, 24). Thus, notwithstanding Kittler's frequent recourse to depth-psychological ideas, the fact remains that his hybrid conceptual paradigm and the depth-psychological approach employed here result in radically diverse interpretations. My own hinges on the inference, based on a pattern of textual evidence, that Gustel unconsciously and magically believes her own femininity to have been responsible for her father's death and that her attachment to the king as a father-substitute is an attempt to "undo" the imagined parricide and its attendant overwhelming guilt by becoming a man (hence, male page) for him. The ultimate object of Gustel's quest is seen here is the real father's love and acceptance. The strategy of masculinity she adopts in pursuit of these implies the profound repression of the hated feminine self. The narrative is viewed, then, as the portrayal of the heroine's symbolic reenactment of the primal father-daughter relationship or, in Freudian terms, her carrying-out of a repetition compulsion.

Kittler's point of departure, by contrast, is that "Gleichwohl ist der leibliche Vater nicht das Ziel des [von Gustels Traum artikulierten] Wunsches. Denn nur darum tritt die Traumrednerin an dessen Platz, um in der Nähe des Königs zu sein, den sie als 'Abgott' und 'Helden' verehrt. . . . Ein lebender, allmächtiger und idealer Vater tritt an die Leerstelle, die der Tod des leibichen aufgetan hat. Der vom Traum artikulierte Wunsch kann also artikuliert werden als das Begehren, anstelle des toten Vaters in der Nähe des idealen zu sein" (p. 194). My central thesis, that Gustel holds herself to blame for her father's death, leads me to conclude that the king is for her a father-imago or transference object over against which she plays out the unconscious drama of guilt and yearning for love. Kittler, who prescinds entirely from the issues of imagined parricide and guilt, views the king as having an autonomous paternal status in Gustel's world, that is, he cannot be said to represent for her anyone but himself in his function as ideal father ("'Abgott' und 'Helden' "). These different premises lead to altogether different readings.

More recently, Christian Sand has made some intriguing speculations on Gustel's dilemma as reflective of Meyer's early childhood experience (*Anomie und Identität: Zur Wirklichkeitsproblematik in der Prosa von C. F. Meyer*, Stuttgarter Arbeiten zur Germanistik no. 79, ed. Ulrich Müller, Franz Hundsnurscher, and Cornelius Sommer [Stuttgart: Hans-Dieter Heinz, 1980], pp. 114–18. Using the analytical techniques of depth psychology and the sociology of knowledge (*Wissenssoziologie*), Sand views Gustel as an expression of Meyer's own Oedipal or even pre-Oedipal conflicts. The inversion of sex, from male author vis-à-vis mother to female protagonist in pursuit of the father-figure, is supposedly intended to defuse the author's own harsh Calvinist ethic which proscribes overt filial gestures of love toward the mother. Sand concludes that "vieles dafür spricht, daß der Page Leubelfing in den ödipalen Identifikationsprozessen [Meyers] seinen Ursprung hat" (p. 115). While he foregoes analysis of the text of *Gustav Adolfs Page,* Sand's biographical hypotheses lend external support to the analysis offered here.

In her excellent article, "Conrad Ferdinand Meyer, Gustav Adolfs Page: Versuch einer Interpretation," Claudia Liver analyzes the tale in terms of its dominant Baroque *teatrum mundi* topos, but is well aware of the tale's essentially modern sensibility as conveyed by the narrator's interpolated comments "deren Inhalt nicht in der Gedankenwelt der mitspielenden Figur lokalisiert werden kann und deren [psychologische] Form ihrer Denkweise widerspricht" (*Annali* 19, no. 3 [1976]: 7–36; quotation from p. 18, note 27). While I take issue with parts of Liver's argument (see, for example, note 26 below), I am in complete accord with her general approach—indeed, my own interpretation may be taken as essentially complementary to hers: while she deals with the fundamental theme of determinism as Meyer styles it in the manifest features of the *teatrum mundi* topos, I attempt to disclose its underlying, occasionally explicit but mainly implicit, psychodynamic dimension.

Periodically through the decades, several other critics have referred to this or that element of the tale's unconscious narrative level, either to leave it at that or to proceed in pursuit of other, peripheral lines of interpretation: thus Hertling: "wie ein Märchentraum wird sein [i.e., Gustel's] so 'kindischer' und langgehegter, dem Bewußtsein zunächst verschlossen bleibender Wunsch [to serve under the king] tatsächlich 'Gestalt gewinnen' " (*Conrad Ferdinand Meyers Epik*, p. 116). Fehr most likely implies the eruption of unconscious motives in Gustel in describing her flight from camp as "eine Flucht vor sich selbst aus einer für sie unerträglich gewordenen Spannung" (*Conrad Ferdinand Meyer*, p. 69). Brückner suggests Gustel's resistance to the repressed when he writes: "Sie ist sich plötzlich bewusst, dass sie ein unnatürliches Dasein führt und nennt sich selbst 'eine Lügnerin, eine Sophistin' " (*Heldengestaltung*, p. 25). Burkhard and Stevens note the covert workings of the unconscious, but only with respect to the king, and even there dismiss the theme as insignificant: "The portrayal of platonic relations between a young girl and a great hero who is ignorant of her sex is, moreover, not a particularly fruitful or significant problem. The association has no more than an unconscious effect on the man, and terminates, in Meyer's account, before any important formative or disruptive effects on the women's character ensue" ("Meyer Reveals Himself," p. 203). Interpreting Gustel's relationship with the king as anything but platonic, Edgar Krebs argues that her dreams signal her unconscious conflict between sexual wish and conscience ("Das Unbewußte in den Dichtungen Conrad Ferdinand Meyers," *Die psychoanalytische Bewegung* 2 [1930]: 336–37). Felix Emmel observes the king's unconscious sensing of Gustel's femaleness and the latter's "eifersüchtiges, unbewußtes Wünschen" (p. 409) with respect to the queen ("Der Eros und der Tod. Zu Conrad Ferdinand Meyers Pagennovelle," *Preussische Jahrbücher* 179 [1920]: 404–15). For Emmel the tale is part of Meyer's complex response to his "späte Pubertätszeit" (p. 408). It should be noted that none of the critics listed here discerns the link between Gustel's noxious relationship to her father, inferable from remarks of the various characters, and her present-time behavior. As stated above, the interpretation offered here is an elucidation of precisely this link.

Finally, there are still other readers who hold other views, prescinding entirely from considerations of the unconscious. Georges Brunet, for example, in his book, *C. F. Meyer et la nouvelle*, sees as the primary issue in *Gustav Adolfs Page*, as in all of Meyer's fiction, that of "des rapports de l'existence humaine et de l'éthique" [Paris: Didier, 1967], p. 269. Brunet's interpretation focuses on what he takes to be the tragic flaws in the king's character, his lust for power and, as standard-bearer of a "just" religious cause, his presumption of invulnerability. On the other hand, both Lily Hohenstein and von Lerber insist on the supposedly innocent, even spiritual quality of Gustel's love as the tale's dominant theme, the former characterizing it as a true "Einklang der Seelen," the latter as "verhalten, keusch, in Zucht genommen" (Hohenstein, *Conrad Ferdinand Meyer* [Bonn: Athenäum, 1957], p. 240; von Lerber, *C. F. Meyer: Der Mensch in der Spannung*, p. 136).

5. In a letter of 9 June 1898 to Fliess, published posthumously in Sigmund Freud, *Aus den Anfängen der Psychoanalyse* (London: Imago, 1950), this according to Frederick J. Beharriell, "C. F. Meyer and the Origins of Psychoanalysis," *Monatshefte* 47 (1955): 142–43. In the psychoanalytic lexicon, deferred action (*Nachträglichkeit*) refers to that behavior performed by an adult in unconscious reaction to an early childhood experience. In Meyer's story Gustel's godfather, Ake Tott, recalls the king's playful fondling and kissing of the infant Gustel and points to this as the basis of her present blind devotion to him. As Beharriell's article (pp. 140–48) demonstrates, the *Anfänge*, a collection of letters and documents written by Freud between 1887 and 1902, contains many references to works by Meyer.

6. Beharriell, "C. F. Meyer and the Origins of Psychoanalysis," p. 148.

7. Ibid.

8. Especially in the older critical literature, *Gustav Adolfs Page* did not fare well. See, for example, Burkhard and Stevens throughout, who find the tale so wanting in virtually every respect that they cannot avoid a concluding admission of having "cruelly analyzed" it ("Meyer Reveals Himself," p. 211); Maync, whose tactful understatement, "Unter seine Meisterwerke ist 'Gustav Adolfs Page' nicht zu rechnen," betrays a similar attitude (*C. F. Meyer und Sein Werk*, p. 212); Emmel, who announces more candidly in his opening sentence, "In der ersten Hälfte des Jahres 1882 schuf Conrad Ferdinand Meyer eine seiner weniger bedeutenden Novellen: 'Gustav Adolfs Page' " ("Der Eros und der Tod," p. 404); and T. de Wyzewa, who throws discretion to the winds in calling the narrative "banale, gauche, puérile" ("Un romancier suisse, Conrad Ferdinand Meyer," *Revue des deux Mondes* 152 [1899]: 938).

At least one current critic agrees with this earlier group. Evans weeds the tale out from those she finds worthy of analysis since "in struktureller Hinsicht ist diese Novelle oft verschwommen und wirkt im Vergleich mit der profilierten Figurenkonstellation im *Heiligen* und der raffinierten Konstruktion verschiedener stofflicher Ebenen und literarischer Anspielungen im *Schuβ von der Kanzel* schemenhaft" (*Formen der Ironie*, p. 6). The present interpretation may be said to defend the tale against the bulk of these assertions, and most vigorously with respect to its alleged lack of a "raffinierten Konstruktion verschiedener stofflicher Ebenen."

9. See James, *Varieties of Religious Experience*, p. 298.

10. As Zeller and Zäch put it in *SW,* 11:279.

11. See, for example, von François's letter of 4 October 1882, in Bettelheim, *François und Meyer: Briefwechsel*, p. 65, and Alfred Zäch, *Conrad Ferdinand Meyer: Dichtkunst als Befreiung aus Lebenshemmnissen* (Frauenfeld: Huber, 1973), pp. 176–77.

12. "Ich las Goethes Egmont und vertiefte mich in den Gedanken: es lohnte wohl, ein Weib zu zeichnen, das ohne Hingabe, ja ohne daβ der Held nur eine Ahnung von ihrem Geschlecht hat, einem hohen Helden in verschwiegener Liebe folgt und für ihn in den Tod geht." Quoted in *SW,* 11:280.

13. Ibid.

14. Burkhard and Stevens, "Meyer Reveals Himself," p. 198.

15. In a letter of 4 July 1882 to Rodenberg, in August Langmesser, ed., *Conrad Ferdinand Meyer und Julius Rodenberg: Ein Briefwechsel* (Berlin: Paetel, 1918), p. 112.

16. Horney, *Feminine Psychology*, p. 74. See also note 3.

17. Ibid., pp. 43–50.

18. See note 5. Although Freud did not publish his theory of the family romance until 1909, the first statement of its main features is contained in a brief essay on Meyer's *Die Richterin* written for Fliess in June of 1898 and first published in the *Anfänge* of 1950 (see Beharriell, "C. F. Meyer and the Origins of Psychoanalysis," pp. 144–45). This essay is generally considered to be the first explicit application of psychoanalysis to a work of literature.

19. To be sure, Freud would later note the power, not only of personal names but even of their individual syllabic components, to arouse incestuous desires. In *Totem and Taboo* (1913), which demonstrates the close parallels between individual compulsive-neurotic behavior and the rigidly observed customs of "primitive" peoples, he discusses, for example, the elaborate precautions taken by the natives of Lepers Island in the New Hebrides to prevent any social contact between brothers and sisters that might expose them to the lures of incest. Prohibitions extend even to the brother's speaking the sister's name aloud: "He will not even mention her name and will guard against using any current word if it forms part of her name. This avoidance, which begins with the ceremony of puberty, is strictly observed for life." See *The Basic Writings of Sigmund Freud*, ed. and trans. A. A. Brill (New York: The Modern Library, 1938), p. 814.

20. The special fascination held by this transitional phase of consciousness for Meyer the lyricist is discussed by Henel, *The Poetry of C. F. Meyer*, p. 30. For its significance in *Das Amulett*, see the previous section, p. 30.

21. See that section of *The Interpretation of Dreams* entitled, "The Work of Displacement," in *The Basic Writings of Sigmund Freud*, pp. 336–39.

22. "Appropriately," that is, in the sense of Freud's observation that punishment dreams characteristically occur "if the thoughts which are day-residues are of a gratifying nature, but express illicit gratifications" (here: the erotic name-coupling reverie immediately preceding sleep). The narrator's remark that Gustel "träumte mit seinem Gewissen" anticipates Freud's singling-out of punishment dreams as a special class in which "it is not the unconscious wish from the repressed material (from the system Ucs. [unconscious]) that is responsible for dreamformation, but the punitive wish reacting against it, a wish pertaining to the ego, even though it is unconscious (i.e., preconscious)." See *The Basic Writings of Sigmund Freud*, p. 504. In a footnote on the same page, added to *The Interpretation of Dreams* in 1930, Freud implies this distinction would have been clearer if he had had at his disposal at the original time of writing "the idea of the super-ego which was later recognized by psychoanalysis."

23. Sigmund Freud, *New Introductory Lectures on Psychoanalysis*, ed. and trans. James Strachey (New York: Norton, 1965), p. 77.

24. See Victoria L. Rippere's excellent article, "Ludwig Tieck's 'Der blonde Eckbert': A Psychological Reading," *PMLA* 85 (1970), 473–86, esp. 484.

25. My translation from the play, in Goethe, *Dramen, Novellen*, vol. 2 of *Goethe Werke* (Frankfurt a. M.: Insel, 1970), p. 202.

26. Critics have been generally stymied by the apparently gratuitous introduction of this *Doppelgängermotiv:* Marianne Burkhard speaks of "the implausible resemblance between Gustel and the duke of Lauenburg" as responsible in part for the work's being "not fully convincing" (*Conrad Ferdinand Meyer,* Twayne's World Authors Series, no. 480, ed. Ulrich Weisstein [Boston: G. K. Hall, 1978], p. 125). Liver regards the motif as one of a number of "unwahrscheinlich anmutenden Elemente" in the tale that have no explanation beyond the fact that they stand "im Dienst einer irrationalistischen Beleuchtung des Schicksals" ("Gustav Adolfs Page," p. 30, number 61). For Zäch, the motif is an absurd contrivance forced upon Meyer by the exigencies of plot: "Und was für Zufälle müssen mitwirken, damit eine Verwechslung des Lauenburgers mit Leubelfing möglich wird!" (*Dichtkunst als Befreiung,* p. 175). Beharriell stands behind Freud's own criticism of the motif as "'an sich so unwahrscheinlich und gar nicht weiter begründet.' Most critics will agree that this complaint is a just one" ("C. F. Meyer and the Origins of Psychoanalysis," pp. 143–44).

The point is, I think, that the resemblance between Gustel and Lauenburg is indeed completely gratuitous in and of itself and takes on meaning only in the context of Gustel's unconscious perception. It is the psychological identification she forms from the resemblance with its fatal consequences that imbues an otherwise irrelevant "accident of nature" with significance. A few critics have attempted to see past the accidental: Kittler, for instance, observes in semiotic terms that "der Doppelgänger [ist] kein bloßes Spiel der Natur und d.h. willkürlich; was ihn ermöglicht, ist das Spiel der Signifikanten, innerhalb dessen die Spiele der Natur erst zählen" (*Der Traum und die Rede,* p. 208). However, beyond our initial agreement that the meaning of the resemblance resides in its meaning-for-Gustel, we have opposite views on what that meaning is: while Kittler argues that "so präsentiert der Doppelgänger der Lauscherin diejenige familiale Position, die sie einnähme, wenn ihr Betrug die Wahrheit wäre" (p. 209), which he consequently interprets as that of rebellious son, a stance shocking to her daughter's attitude of "Idolatrie" (p. 210), I assert conversely that it is the lethal *daughter,* concealed behind the doubleganger's correspondingly docile male façade, which Gustel unconsciously and symbolically (mis)perceives and to which she reacts with shock by virtue of her identification with it. For Wiesmann the element of recognition so shocking to Gustel is Lauenburg's adulterous liaison with Corinna, an unconscious reminder of her own illicit desires with respect to the king: "Nur läßt der Lauenburger seinen Trieben freien Lauf, während sich der Page keusch zurückhält (*Dichter des Todes,* p. 148). This is seconded by Brückner: "Ihr Doppelgänger, der Lauenburger, führt in seinem Verhältnis zu Corinna das aus, worauf Auguste im Unterbewusstsein hofft" (*Heldengestaltung,* p. 25). The view here, however, is that Gustel is not held back by the fear of violating conventional sanctions against adultery, or at least not primarily by such fear, but rather that she is gripped by the far more primal terror that any feminine overtures might again result in parricide.

27. The foregoing arguments may serve as a response to Burkhard and Stevens, who consider Gustel's sudden flight and "the King's lack of interest in Gustel's action and whereabouts" to be among "the least convincing elements in the story" ("Meyer Reveals Himself," pp. 195–96). Indeed, if one neglects to take the unconscious dimension of the narrative into account, these elements have little or no comprehensible basis.

28. The motif of the surge of enormous physical strength resulting from the despair of conscience, enabling a woman to lift a burden far beyond her normal capacity, fascinated Meyer. As Hertling notes, the motif informs the central background legend of the cross-bearing duchess in *Plautus im Nonnenkloster,* the penitent founder of the cloister "deren 'Gewissen . . . Gott . . . gerührt' hatte . . ., ja die infolgedessen das echte Kreuz 'gehoben haben . . . mochte . . . mit den Riesenkräften der Verzweiflung und der Inbrunst'" (*Conrad Ferdinand Meyers Epik,* p. 115).

29. Meyer, *Briefe,* 1:33.

30. Quoted in W. P. Bridgwater, "C. F. Meyer and Nietzsche," *Modern Language Review* 60 (1965): 579.

31. I cannot agree with Hertling, who takes Meyer's phrase "Leben der Gegenwart" to refer to his own personal dreamlife, hence a kind of present-time autobiographical well from which he supposedly drew to personalize the remote characters and events of history (*Conrad Ferdinand Meyers Epik,* p. 201). No doubt Meyer did this, but he was surely not referring to this creative use of his own dreams in the above-quoted pronouncement on the challenge of historical fiction. The expression "Leben der Gegenwart" clearly implies the general intellec-

tual-cultural milieu in which Meyer found himself and cannot be reduced to the narrow intrapsychic sphere of Hertling's hypothesis. Moreover, the source of the pronouncement in Vischer's aesthetics, where Meyer's "Leben der Gegenwart" is unquestionably seen to derive from the former's "Bewegungen der Gegenwart" and "der geistigen Welt derjenigen, für die er darstellt," leaves no doubt as to the broad, collective scope of the expression.

32. A political strategy vigorously pursued, in fact, by Freud himself and the early Vienna circle. See Frank J. Sulloway's brilliant *Freud, Biologist of the Mind: Beyond the Psychoanalytic Legend* (New York: Basic Books, 1979).

33. See, in addition to Sulloway (*Freud, Biologist of the Mind*, p. 146), Henri F. Ellenberger, *The Discovery of the Unconscious: The History and Evolution of Dynamic Psychiatry* (New York: Basic Books, 1970), esp. chapters 4, "The Background of Dynamic Psychiatry," and 5, "On the Threshold of a New Dynamic Psychiatry." Much of the intellectual-historical background discussion that follows draws on the findings of these two monumental studies.

34. Sulloway, *Freud, Biologist of the Mind*, pp. 252–54.

35. Ellenberger, *Discovery of the Unconscious*, pp. 208–09.

36. Quoted in and translated by Ellenberger, *Discovery of the Unconscious*, p. 209.

37. Ibid. See Thomas Mann, *Freud und die Zukunft* (Vienna: Bormann-Fischer, 1936).

38. See Franz G. Alexander and Sheldon T. Selesnick, *The History of Psychiatry: An Evaluation of Psychiatric Thought and Practice from Prehistoric Times to the Present* (New York: Harper & Row, 1966), pp. 169–70.

39. Although no discussion of the pre-Freudian concept of the unconscious can be considered complete that does not take Nietzsche into account, he is nevertheless omitted from the present discussion since there is no evidence of Meyer's having had any acquaintance with his writings prior to 1887, five years after the publication of *Gustav Adolfs Page*. According to Bridgwater, "The *only* work of Nietzsche's that Meyer is *known* to have read is *Jenseits von Gut and Böse* (1886)" ("C. F. Meyer and Nietzsche," p. 569; emphasis Bridgwater's).

40. Bettelheim, *François und Meyer: Briefwechsel*, p. 22.

41. Bridgwater, "C. F. Meyer and Nietzsche," p. 571.

42. Quoted in and translated by Ellenberger, *Discovery of the Unconscious*, p. 505.

43. Sulloway, *Freud, Biologist of the Mind*, p. 253.

44. Ellenberger, *Discovery of the Unconscious*, p. 210; Alexander and Selesnick, *History of Psychiatry*, p. 170. For a detailed and subtle exposition of Hartmann's system, see Dennis N. Kenedy Darnoi, *The Unconscious and Eduard von Hartmann* (The Hague: Martinus Nijhoff, 1967), esp. Chapters 3, "Discovery and Realm of Operation of the Unconscious," and 4, "Division and Kinds of the Unconscious."

45. Bridgwater, "C. F. Meyer and Nietzsche," p. 570.

46. Meyer, *Briefe*, 1 : 84.

47. Quoted in Kenneth Hughes's review of *Tagebücher 1935–1936*, by Thomas Mann, ed. Peter de Mendelssohn, *German Quarterly* 53 (1980): 251.

48. Ellenberger, *Discovery of the Unconscious*, p. 210.

49. See p. 30.

50. Ellenberger, *Discovery of the Unconscious*, pp. 218–20.

51. Ibid., pp. 220–21.

52. Frey, *Leben und Werke*, pp. 274.

53. Ellenberger, *Discovery of the Unconscious*, pp. 222–23.

54. So much so that the dependency was worthy of a book-length treatment. See the previously cited *Women in the Life and Art of Conrad Ferdinand Meyer* by Lena Dahme. See also Emmel, "Der Eros und der Tod," pp. 406–07.

55. For a discussion of what I believe to be a largely misunderstood relationship—that between Meyer and his mother—see my "Lena Dahme contra Psychobiographical Character Assassination: Towards the 'Rehabilitation' of Frau Betsy Meyer," *German Life and Letters* 36 (1983): 294–300.

56. Frey, *Leben und Werke*, p. 51.

57. Ellenberger, *Discovery of the Unconscious*, pp. 295–96.

58. In addition to Ranke's *Französische Geschichte*, mentioned in the discussion of *Das Amulett* in part 1, Meyer had also read Michelet's *Histoire de France au seizième siècle*, tome 9, *Guerres de religion* (Paris, 1856), in researching the historical background for his first novella. See Meyer, *Briefe*, 1 : 32, and *SW*, 11 : 226.

59. Ellenberger, *Discovery of the Unconscious,* p. 296.

60. See, in addition to the comprehensive *Histoire de France,* the earlier panegyric, *Le peuple* (1846).

61. Frey, *Leben und Werke,* p. 51.

62. Ellenberger, *Discovery of the Unconscious,* p. 277.

63. For concise accounts of the impact of Vischer's theories on Meyer's early Pietism, see Karl Emanuel Lusser, *Conrad Ferdinand Meyer. Das Problem seiner Jugend* (Leipzig: Haessel, 1926), p. 52, and Dahme, *Women in the Life,* pp. 24–25.

64. In a letter of 24 June 1885 to François Wille, Meyer mentions that "Ich lese eben Paradoxe von Max Nordau, das Sie wohl auch durchblättern" (*Briefe,* 1:177). Undoubtedly by this time Meyer had also read, or at least knew of, Nordau's *Die konventionellen Lügen der Kulturmenschheit,* which was published the year before *Paradoxe* and the year after *Gustav Adolfs Page* and created something of a sensation throughout the German-speaking countries and America with its unflinching diatribe on the hypocrisy of contemporary social institutions. One wonders if the poet noticed how uncannily the social-conspiracy theme in the epilogue chapter of *Page* anticipates this harangue of Nordau's, which contains essays with such titles as "The Lie of a Monarchy and Aristocracy," "The Political Lie," and "The Lie of Religion."

65. See note 39.

66. The earlier judgment in a letter of 6 February 1874 to J. R. Rahn, the later in a letter of 10 June 1889, to his publisher Haessel, taken from *Briefe,* 1:240, and 2:172, respectively.

67. Meyer, *Briefe,* 2:290.

68. Meyer, *Briefe,* 1:176.

69. Ibid. The novel's first appearance in German translation in 1882 to almost immediate acclaim certainly stokes one's curiosity about its possible prominence in Meyer's imagination at that time. See V. V. Dudkin, "Dostoevskij v nemetskoy kritike (1882–1925)," in *Dostoevskij v zarubezhnykh literaturakh,* ed. B. G. Reizov (Leningrad: Nauka, 1978), p. 175; also Ernst Hauswedell, "Die Kenntnis von Dostojewsky und seinem Werke im deutschen Naturalismus und der Einfluß seines 'Raskolnikoff' auf die Epoche von 1880–95" (Diss., Munich, 1924), p. 13.

70. Meyer, *Briefe,* 1:79.

71. In a letter to his philosopher friend Baader, quoted in Ricarda Huch, *Die Romantik: Blütezeit, Ausbreitung und Verfall* (Tübingen: Rainer Wunderlich, 1951), p. 81.

72. The letter, in *Briefe,* 1:188, is dated 3 March 1887.

73. Meyer, *Briefe,* 1:429.

74. Emphasis Bridgwater's, "C. F. Meyer and Nietzsche," p. 574. More recently, Merian-Genast put this view in more global terms in arguing that "Meyers Kunst ersteht aus der Flucht vor der Wirklichkeit und ist Ersatz für ein ungelebtes Leben" (*Die Gestalt des Künstlers,* p. 14).

75. Only the private therapeutic sanctuary provided by Dr. Charles Borrel at Préfargier following the breakdown could induce Meyer to share with another person some of the problems underlying his emotional illness, such as his troubled relationship with his father, a successful but aloof academic who suddenly died when Meyer was fifteen (a contributory stimulus for the psychological themes of parricide and paternal abandonment in *Gustav Adolfs Page?*). Arthur Kielholz cites evidence from Dr. Borrel's files of the floundering, careerless son's angry outbursts against the father with whose ghost he apparently felt himself in anguished competition ("Conrad Ferdinand Meyer und seine Beziehungen zu Königsfelden," *Monatsschrift für Psychiatrie und Neurologie* 109 [1944]: 272). But not a hint of any of this in the letters, not even those written at the safe remove of decades.

76. Meyer, *Briefe,* 1:411.

CHAPTER 3. UNCONSCIOUSNESS IN TERMS OF LAPSARIAN MYTH IN *DAS LEIDEN EINES KNABEN*

1. In a letter of 31 August 1806 to Otto August Rühle von Lilienstern, in Heinrich von Kleist, *Briefe 1805–1811,* vol. 7 of *dtv-Gesamtausgabe* (Munich: Deutscher Taschenbuch Verlag, 1964), p. 24.

2. Several commentators have noted the prominence of Edenic and lapsarian allusion in the tale: for example, David Jackson, who observes that Julian and Mirabelle "seem for a moment

like Adam and Eve in Paradise" ("Shadows on the Face of the Sun King: C. F. Meyer's *Das Leiden eines Knaben* and Hippolyte Taine's *Les origines de la France Contemporaine*," *Revue de Littérature Comparée* 51 [1977]: 417–31, quotation from p. 428); Hertling, who emphasizes throughout the association between the Royal Botanical Gardens and the Garden of Paradise (*Conrad Ferdinand Meyers Epik*, pp. 124–30); Reinhardt, who avers that "Edenic imagery is of cardinal importance in *Das Leiden eines Knaben*" ("Wordplays," p. 53); Brückner, *Heldengestaltung*, pp. 52–53; and Per Øhrgaard, who sees Fagon, interestingly, as a lapsed version of Julian: "er ist Julian nach dem Sündenfall, Julian, der Partei ergriffen hat" (*C. F. Meyer: Zur Entwicklung seiner Thematik*, Det Kongelige Danske Videnskabernes Selskab, Historisk-filosofiske Meddelelser 43, 2 [Copenhagen: Munksgaard, 1969], p. 88). No one, however, has heretofore traced lapsarian allusion throughout as a comprehensive principle of thematic structure, nor interpreted it conceptually in the terms presented here.

The autobiographical element, so strong in *Das Leiden eines Knaben*, is nicely elucidated by M. Burkhard, *Conrad Ferdinand Meyer*, pp. 126–29; Carlo Moos, *Dasein als Erinnerung: Conrad Ferdinand Meyer und die Geschichte*, Geist und Werk der Zeiten 35, ed. Rudolf von Albertini et al (Bern: Herbert Lang, 1973), p. 81; and Gerhart Binder, "Conrad Ferdinand Meyers Novelle: 'Das Leiden eines Knaben,'" *Deutschunterricht* 3, no. 2 (1951): 64–72.

Other, interesting insights and observations are offered by Karl Fehr, who sees Mouton as administering a kind of "Beschäftigungstherapie" to Julian through the painting lessons (*Conrad Ferdinand Meyer; Auf- und Niedergang seiner dichterischen Produktivität im Spannungsfeld von Erbanlagen und Umwelt* [Bern: Francke, 1983], p. 267); Evans, who reads the tale as structured according to a principle of "Pluralismus der Sprache," by which she basically means the Babel-like variability of linguistic style and intent among the characters, all this issuing "aus einer ironischen Grundabsicht des Dichters" (*Formen der Ironie*, pp. 77–99; quotation from p. 77); Sand, who, operating from the perspective of *Wissenssoziologie*, offers a fascinating view of the tale as a scathing portrayal of the Byzantine legal and moral subterfuges so often devised by cultures for getting rid of undesirable individuals (*Anomie und Identität*, pp. 236–47); Kittler, specialist in *Kommunikationstheorie*, who sees the tale as an exposition of the tragic consequences for the linguistically deficient Julian, "der schöne Stumpfsinnige," of his exclusion from the universe of discourse: "Der Pakt der Kommunikation, der alle anderen ermöglicht, wird gebrochen: zwischen Vater und Sohn, zwischen den Patres und dem Vater, zwischen ihnen und dem Sohn" (*Der Traum und die Rede*, pp. 172–93; quotation from p. 192); and W. D. Williams, one of the first critics to point out the significance of the frame (*The Stories of C. F. Meyer* [Oxford: Clarendon, 1962], pp. 70–84); along with several other commentators whose arguments are taken up in detail below in connection with my own.

3. This may at first glance seem to contradict the account in Genesis of Adam and Eve's awakening upon eating of the Tree of Knowledge ("Then the eyes of both were opened," [Gen. 3 : 7]), but it soon becomes clear that Meyer's version of the Fall is simply the other side of the Genesis "coin" and is perfectly consonant with the prototype. Adam and Eve's awakening in Genesis is to themselves ("and they became aware of their nakedness," [Gen. 3 : 7]), which entails an awareness of their separateness from the rest of creation. The birth of self-consciousness is thus the death of primal consciousness, i.e., of that direct apprehension of and communion with creation that was Paradise. It is this loss of the primal delight in creation—the price of the awakening to self—that is the focus of the lapsarian myth in *Das Leiden eines Knaben*.

4. Apparently the court patois itself had not been much purged since Scudéry's time. Jackson points out the cue Meyer took from Taine in depicting the suffocatingly artificial and sterile character of the language still spoken at the court of Louis XIV ("Shadows," pp. 428–29).

5. The necessary obverse of the sinister awareness of being watched, i.e., watching, particularly in the sense of spying or eavesdropping, has been identified by many as a prominent motif in Meyer's tales. See, for example, Kittler, *Der Traum, und die Rede*, p. 203, esp. note 1; Williams, *Stories*, pp. 37, 207–09; and Wiesmann, *Dichter des Todes*, p. 115.

6. For example, Manfred R. Jacobson calls him "a retarded boy" and elsewhere refers to his "stunted mind" ("The King and the Court Jester: A Reading of C. F. Meyer's *Das Leiden eines Knaben*," *Seminar* 15 [1979]: pp. 36, 28); Reinhardt speaks of his "slow-wittedness" ("Wordplays," p. 51); and Williams imputes to Fagon the judgment of Julian as "clearly mentally retarded" (*Stories*, p. 75).

7. Kleist, *dtv-Gesamtausgabe*, 5 : 77.

8. Ibid.

9. Ibid., p. 74. It is interesting to note that both Kleist and Meyer suffered a great deal from shyness and a consequent inarticulateness in social situations. Kleist, in fact, is said to have stammered. Undoubtedly, the preoccupation of both authors with the theme of inhibiting self-awareness is deeply rooted in painful personal experience. On the other hand, Meyer was, like Julian, an excellent fencer in his youth.

10. Or, as Rousseau himself delightfully puts it in describing his own early schooling in Geneva, "Latin and all that sorry nonsense as well that goes by the name of education," in *The Confessions of Jean-Jacques Rousseau*, trans. J. M. Cohen (New York: Penguin, 1982), p. 23.

11. In the wistful phrase of August Wilhelm Schlegel, *Schriften* (Munich: Goldmann, n.d.), p. 169.

12. E. T. A. Hoffmann, *Hoffmans Werke*, ed. Viktor Schweizer and Paul Zaunert (Leipzig: Bibliographisches Institut, n.d.), 1 : 12.

13. Ibid., 1 : 68.

14. It is singularly appropriate that Kleist's "Über das Marionettentheater" has been included in a volume on Zen Buddhism as an example of "Universal Zen." See Nancy Wilson Ross, ed., *The World of Zen: An East-West Anthology* (New York: Random House, 1960), pp. 293–99.

15. Fagon's act of storytelling, although primarily a structural device, may of course also be regarded thematically as an instance of verbal art. As I endeavor to point out in the same discussion later on, it fares no better than Molière's comedy in the overall scheme of the work.

16. Hoffmann, *Hoffmanns Werke*, 1 : 67.

17. The artificial refinement of the classical French spoken at court with its rigid proscription of the sort of colorful, earthy idiom favored by, for instance, Mimeure, Mouton, and D'Argenson is another facet of the anti-language theme, further illustrating the putative tendency of language to seduce and insulate man from reality. See Jackson, "Shadows," pp. 428–30. Evans is quite right in her assertion that "In keiner anderen Novelle von C. F. Meyer ist Sprache ein so dringendes und zentrales Anliegen wie im *Leiden eines Knaben*" (*Formen der Ironie*, p. 79). Elsewhere she observes that "Meyers Sprachskepsis tiefe Spuren in diesem Werk hinterlassen hat" and that the tale's point of view on language is that "mit Sprache lässt sich nur auf Umwegen und auch dann nur bedingt an die Wahrheit herankommen, weil eben auch letztere nur subjektiv erfahrbar ist" (p. 97). I agree with Evans up to that final *weil* clause: in the present discussion I attempt to show that the Garden community stands precisely for the possibility, however remote, of a perfect apprehension of "Wahrheit," one transcending the constraints of language and hence also the subject-object split in which language is grounded. The Garden community represents emancipation from an imprisoning solipsism. Had Evans noticed the Edenic-mythic significance of the Garden, she might well have concurred.

18. Reinhardt, "Wordplays," p. 53.

19. Kleist, *dtv-Gesamtausgabe*, 5 : 77–78 and 74.

20. Novalis, *Werke*, 3d ed. (Hamburg: Hoffmann & Campe, 1966), p. 148.

21. Thomas Merton, *Conjectures of a Guilty Bystander* (Garden City, N.Y.: Image, 1968), p. 307.

22. Ibid., pp. 307–08.

23. Thus, for example, Reinhardt, "Wordplays," p. 53.

24. Two classic treatments of the subject, both dating around the turn of the century, are Richard M. Bucke's *Cosmic Consciousness: A Study in the Evolution of the Human Mind* (1900; reprint, New York: Causeway, 1974) and the previously cited *Varieties of Religious Experience* by William James. In a long introduction Bucke describes the main features of the shift from simple to self-consciousness and thence to cosmic consciousness, postulating each state as a discrete and fundamental step on the human evolutionary ladder. James is especially brilliant in his analysis of the conversion experience (lectures 9 and 10), viewing it as he does from both ends, that is, both to and away from religion. Both books are replete with fascinating auto biographical case-histories.

25. Kleist, *dtv-Gesamtausgabe*, 5 : 75.

26. Anselmus' arduous apprenticeship to Archivarius Lindhorst, which is the Romantic poet's rite of passage to the Transcendent, could stand as a mythic equivalent of Bucke's discursive analysis of the phenomenon of cosmic consciousness (see note 24). For Hoffmann

this sublime condition, achieved by so few, is nothing other than "das Leben in der Poesie, der sich der heilige Einklang aller Wesen als tiefstes Geheimnis der Natur offenbaret" (*Hoffmanns Werke*, 1 : 103). Here poetry is ultimately a post-verbal consciousness-transforming revelation.

27. Schlegel, *Schriften*, p. 165.

28. Notwithstanding the expulsion of the Jesuits from France in 1880, Reinhardt seems unaccountably severe in his judgment that "He [Meyer] could well afford to consider himself generous towards the Jesuits" ("Wordplays," p. 52, note 20).

29. In Dostoevsky, *Notes from Underground*, pt. 1, chap. 9. Evans has also recognized Julian's Christlike attributes. See *Formen der Ironie*, p. 98 and esp. p. 153, note 35.

30. Act 2, scene 6, in Molière, *Le Malade imaginaire*, ed. Everett Ward Olmsted (New York: Ginn, 1905), p. 85.

31. See, for example, Michel Foucault, *Discipline and Punish: The Birth of the Prison*, trans. Alan Sheridan (New York: Vintage, 1979), esp. pp. 102–03.

32. One wonders, inevitably, how strongly Meyer himself actually did doubt the ability of linguistic, and hence his own, art to "get out of its own skin," i.e., to transcend its own social conditioning. That his doubts on this score may well have been considerable is supported by the implications of Martin Swales's comments on the function of the frame in *Das Leiden eines Knaben*: "Meyer uses the 'Rahmen' to express devastating doubts about the value of art, about its ability to have any decisive effect on the real world at which it is directed. . . . Fagon's story [his 'narrative art'] does not work: it is powerless before the corruption, nastiness, and bigotry of the social world, it is unable to modify the consciousness of its hearers" ("Fagon's Defeat: Some Remarks on C. F. Meyer's *Das Leiden eines Knaben*," *Germanic Review* 52 [1977]: 42–43). Could this be because the consciousness of the storyteller, however well-intentioned, remains itself unmodified in some subtle but essential way, being as deeply woven into the fabric of the self-conscious society as that of the man whose villainy he would expose? See the discussion of Fagon's character below. Swales quotes a telling sentence from a letter of Meyer's, which I also append here: "Wo die Kunst die Leidenschaft reinigt, d.h. der Mensch sich selbst beruhigt und begnügt, entsteht die Vorstellung einer trügerischen Einheit, während wir (und so photographiert uns auch die realistische Kunst) doch so gründlich zwiespältig [self-conscious?] und nur durch ein anderes als wir, durch Gott, zu heilen sind" (p. 42).

33. On the issue of Julian's death I can only agree with Reinhardt's judgment against Karl Fehr: "Karl Fehr's discovery of justice and divine grace in Julian's death exemplifies the well-meaning but wrongheaded tendency of high-minded Meyer exegetes to translate the negative into the positive" ("Wordplays," p. 59). See Karl Fehr, *Der Realismus in der schweizerischen Literatur* (Bern: Francke, 1965), p. 241. The same "wrongheaded" optimism misleads Øhrgaard in his interpretation of Fagon's closing remark: "Fagon hat die irdische Gerechtigkeit in Bewegung bringen wollen, hat versucht, den König zu engagieren. Als er die Vergeblichkeit seines Versuchs einsieht, deutet er seine Niederlage in einen Sieg um: der König könne getrost essen, am Ende habe der unglückliche Julian doch gesiegt.—Die irdische Gerechtigkeit war nicht mehr sichtbar, und Meyer mußte versuchen, das Geschehen selber als sinnvoll zu interpretieren" (*Zur Entwicklung*, p. 88).

34. Swales, "Fagon's Defeat," p. 30.

35. Jacobson, "The King," p. 27. Jacobson's first footnote, p. 27, contains a succinct review of the judgments of previous critics on the function and merit of the frame, dividing them up between the earlier skeptics and the more recent advocates.

36. Sjaak Onderdelinden also detects a self-interested motive in Fagon's storytelling: not that of confession and forgiveness but of "Selbstrechtfertigung." See *Die Rahmenerzählungen Conrad Ferdinand Meyers*, Germanistisch-anglistische Reihe der Universität Leiden 13, ed. C. Soeteman, A. G. H. Bachrach, and J. G. Kooij (Leiden: Universitaire pers Leiden, 1974), pp. 61–62.

37. Tieck's *Der blonde Eckbert* is a masterly depiction of the unconscious resentment borne by the penitent for his confessor.

38. In his recent book, *The Great Code: The Bible and Literature* (New York: Harcourt Brace Jovanovich, 1981).

39. In this aspect of his theme Meyer again seems to prefigure the thought of Foucault, who put the elusive issue of power this way: "The question of power remains a total enigma. Who exercises power? And in what sphere? We now know with reasonable certainty who exploits

others, who receives the profits, which people are involved, and we know how these funds are reinvested. But as for power . . . [sic] We know that it is not in the hands of those who govern. . . . It is often difficult to say who holds power in a precise sense, but it is easy to see who lacks power." See Michel Foucault, *Language, Counter-memory, Practice: Selected Essays and Interviews*, ed. Donald F. Bouchard, trans. Donald F. Bouchard and Sherry Simon (Ithaca: Cornell Univ. Press, 1977), p. 213.

Bibliography

Alexander, Franz G., and Sheldon T. Selesnick. *The History of Psychiatry: An Evaluation of Psychiatric Thought and Practice from Prehistoric Times to the Present.* New York: Harper & Row, 1966.

Beharriell, Frederick J. "C. F. Meyer and the Origins of Psychoanalysis." *Monatshefte* 47 (1955): 140–48.

Berlin, Isaiah. *The Hedgehog and the Fox: An Essay on Tolstoy's View of History.* New York: Touchstone, 1953.

Bettelheim, Anton, ed. *Louise von François und Conrad Ferdinand Meyer: Ein Briefwechsel.* 2d ed. Berlin: VWV, 1920.

Binder, Gerhart. "Conrad Ferdinand Meyers Novelle: 'Das Leiden eines Knaben.'" *Deutschunterricht* 3, no. 2 (1951): 64–72.

Blankenagel, John C. "Conrad Ferdinand Meyer: *Das Amulett.*" *Journal of English and Germanic Philology* 33 (1934): 270–79.

Bridgwater, W. P. "C. F. Meyer and Nietzsche." *Modern Language Review* 60 (1965): 568–83.

Brinkmann, Richard, ed. *Begriffsbestimmung des literarischen Realismus.* Wege der Forschung, 212. Darmstadt: Wissenschaftliche Buchgesellschaft, 1969.

———. *Wirklichkeit und Illusion: Studien über Gehalt und Grenzen des Begriffs Realismus für die erzählende Dichtung des neunzehnten Jahrhunderts.* Tübingen: Niemeyer, 1957.

Brückner, Hans-Dieter. *Heldengestaltung im Prosawerk Conrad Ferdinand Meyers.* Europäische Hochschulschriften: Deutsche Literatur und Germanistik, series 1, 38. Bern: Herbert Lang, 1970.

Brunet, Georges. *C. F. Meyer et la nouvelle.* Paris: Didier, 1967.

Bucke, Richard M. *Cosmic Consciousness: A Study in the Evolution of the Human Mind.* 1900. Reprint. New York: Causeway, 1974.

Burkhard, Arthur. *Conrad Ferdinand Meyer: The Style and the Man.* Cambridge: Harvard University Press, 1932.

Burkhard, Arthur, and Henry H. Stevens. "Conrad Ferdinand Meyer Reveals Himself: A Critical Examination of 'Gustav Adolfs Page.'" *Germanic Review* 15 (1940): 191–212.

Burkhard, Marianne. *Conrad Ferdinand Meyer.* Twayne's World Authors Series, 480. Edited by Ulrich Weisstein. Boston: G. K. Hall, 1978.

Clark, James M. Introduction to *Das Amulett,* by Conrad Ferdinand Meyer. Edited by James M. Clark. London: T. Nelson, 1955.

Cromphout, Gustaaf van. "Emerson and the Dialectics of History." *PMLA* 91 (1976): 54–65.

Crookall, Robert. *The Study and Practice of Astral Projection.* 1960. Reprint. Secaucus, N.J.: Citadel, 1976.

Dahme, Lena F. *Women in the Life and Art of Conrad Ferdinand Meyer.* 1936. Reprint. New York: AMS Press, 1966.

Darnoi, Dennis M. Kenedy. *The Unconscious and Eduard von Hartmann.* The Hague: Martinus Nijhoff, 1967.

Dudkin, V. V. "Dostoevskij v nemetskoy kritike (1882–1925)." In *Dostoevskij v zarubezhnykh literaturakh,* edited by B. G. Reizov, pp. 175–219. Leningrad: Nauka, 1978.

Ellenberger, Henri F. *The Discovery of the Unconscious: The History and Evolution of Dynamic Psychiatry.* New York: Basic Books, 1970.

Emmel, Felix. "Der Eros und der Tod. Zu Conrad Ferdinand Meyers Pagennovelle." *Preussische Jahrbücher* 179 (1920): 404–15.

Ermatinger, Emil. "Eine Quelle zu C. F. Meyers Novelle 'Gustav Adolfs Page.'" *Das literarische Echo* 19 (1916): 22–26.

Evans, Tamara S. *Formen der Ironie in Conrad Ferdinand Meyers Novellen.* Bern: Francke, 1980.

Fehr, Karl. *Conrad Ferdinand Meyer.* Stuttgart: Metzler, 1971.

———. *Conrad Ferdinand Meyer: Auf- und Niedergang seiner dichterischen Produktivität im Spannungsfeld von Erbanlagen und Umwelt.* Bern: Francke, 1983.

———. *Der Realismus in der schweizerischen Literatur.* Bern: Francke, 1965.

Feise, Ernst. "Fatalismus als Grundzug von Conrad Ferdinand Meyers Werken." *Euphorion* 17 (1910): 111–43. Reprinted in *Xenion,* pp. 180–214. Baltimore: Johns Hopkins University Press, 1950.

Feise, Ernst, and Harry Steinhauer, eds. *German Literature since Goethe.* Vol. 1. Boston: Houghton Mifflin, 1958.

Foucault, Michel. *Discipline and Punish: The Birth of the Prison.* Translated by Alan Sheridan. New York: Vintage, 1979.

———. *Language, Counter-memory, Practice: Selected Essays and Interviews.* Translated by Donald F. Bouchard and Sherry Simon. Edited by Donald F. Bouchard. Ithaca: Cornell University Press, 1977.

Freud, Sigmund. *Aus den Anfängen der Psychoanalyse*. London: Imago, 1950.

———. *New Introductory Lectures on Psychoanalysis*. Translated and edited by James Strachey. New York: Norton, 1965.

———. *The Basic Writings of Sigmund Freud*. Translated and edited by A. A. Brill. New York: The Modern Library, 1938.

Frey, Adolf. *Conrad Ferdinand Meyer: Sein Leben und seine Werke*. 2d ed. Stuttgart: Cotta, 1909.

Frye, Northrop. *The Great Code: The Bible and Literature*. New York: Harcourt Brace Jovanovich, 1981.

Goethe, Johann Wolfgang. *Dramen, Novellen*. Vol. 2 of *Goethe Werke*. Frankfurt a.M.: Insel, 1970.

Hauswedell, Ernst. "Die Kenntnis von Dostojewsky und seinem Werke im deutschen Naturalismus und der Einfluß seines 'Raskolnikoff' auf die Epoche von 1880–95." Diss., Munich, 1924.

Henel, Heinrich. *The Poetry of Conrad Ferdinand Meyer*. Madison: University of Wisconsin Press, 1954.

Hertling, Gunter H. *Conrad Ferdinand Meyers Epik: Traumbeseelung, Traumbesinnung und Traumbesitz*. Bern: Francke, 1973.

———. "Religiosität ohne Vorurteil: Zum Wendepunkt in C. F. Meyers 'Das Amulett.' " *Zeitschrift für Deutsche Philologie* 90 (1971): 526–45.

Hoffmann, E. T. A. *Hoffmanns Werke*. Vol. 1. Edited by Viktor Schweizer and Paul Zaunert. Leipzig: Bibliographisches Institut, n.d.

Hohenstein, Lily. *Conrad Ferdinand Meyer*. Bonn: Athenäum, 1957.

Horney, Karen. *Feminine Psychology*. Translated by Edward R. Clemmens, John M. Meth, Edward Schattner, and Gerda F. Willner. Edited by Harold Kelman. New York: Norton, 1973.

Huber, Walter. *Stufen dichterischer Selbstdarstellung in C. F. Meyers* Amulett *und* Jürg Jenatsch. Europäische Hochschulschriften: Deutsche Sprache und Literatur, series 1, 340. Las Vegas: Peter Lang, 1979.

Huch, Ricarda. *Die Romantik: Blütezeit, Ausbreitung und Verfall*. Tübingen: Rainer Wunderlich, 1951.

Hughes, Kenneth. Reivew of *Tagebücher 1935–36*, by Thomas Mann. Edited by Peter de Mendelssohn. *German Quarterly* 53 (1980): 251.

Jackson, D. A. "Recent Meyer Criticism: New Avenues or Cul-de-sac?" *Revue des Langues Vivantes* 34 (1968): 620–36.

———. "Schadau, the Satirized Narrator, in C. F. Meyer's *Das Amulett*." *Trivium* 7 (1972): 61–69.

———. "Shadows on the Face of the Sun King: C. F. Meyer's *Das Leiden eines Knaben* and Hippolyte Taine's *Les origines de la France Contemporaine*." *Revue de Littérature Comparée* 51 (1977): 417–31.

Jacobson, Manfred R. "The King and the Court Jester: A Reading of C. F. Meyer's *Das Leiden eines Knaben*." *Seminar* 15 (1979): 27–38.

James, William. *The Varieties of Religious Experience: A Study in Human Nature*. New York: Mentor, 1958.

Kielholz, Arthur. "Conrad Ferdinand Meyer und seine Beziehungen zu Königsfelden." *Monatsschrift für Psychiatrie und Neurologie* 109 (1944): 257–89.

Kittler, Friedrich. *Der Traum und die Rede: Eine Analyse der Kommunikationssituation Conrad Ferdinand Meyers*. Bern: Francke, 1977.

Kleist, Heinrich von. *dtv-Gesamtausgabe*. Vols. 5 and 7. Munich: Deutscher Taschenbuch Verlag, 1964.

Krebs, Edgar. "Das Unbewußte in den Dichtungen Conrad Ferdinand Meyers." *Die psychoanalytische Bewegung* 2 (1930): 336–37.

Langmesser, August, ed. *Conrad Ferdinand Meyer und Julius Rodenberg: Ein Briefwechsel*. Berlin: Paetel, 1918.

Leopold, Keith. "Meyer and Mérimée: A Study of Conrad Ferdinand Meyer's *Das Amulett* and its Relationship to Prosper Mérimée's *Chronique du règne de Charles IX*." *University of Queensland Papers* 1 (1960): 1–13.

Lerber, Helene von. *Conrad Ferdinand Meyer: Der Mensch in der Spannung*. Basel: Reinhardt, 1949.

Liver, Claudia. "Conrad Ferdinand Meyer, Gustav Adolfs Page: Versuch einer Interpretation." *Annali* 19, no. 3 (1976): 7–36.

Lusser, Karl Emanuel. *Conrad Ferdinand Meyer. Das Problem seiner Jugend*. Leipzig: Haessel, 1926.

Mann, Thomas. *Freud und die Zukunft*. Vienna: Bormann-Fischer, 1936.

Martini, Fritz. *Deutsche Literatur im bürgerlichen Realismus, 1848–1898*. 3d ed. Stuttgart: Metzler, 1974.

Maync, Harry. *Conrad Ferdinand Meyer und sein Werk*. 1925. Reprint. New York: AMS, 1969.

McCort, Dennis. "Historical Consciousness versus Action in C. F. Meyer's *Das Amulett*." *Symposium* 32 (1978): 114–32.

―――. "Lena Dahme contra Psychobiographical Character Assassination: Towards the 'Rehabilitation' of Frau Betsy Meyer." *German Life and Letters* 36 (1983): 294–300.

Merian-Genast, Christine. *Die Gestalt des Künstlers im Werk Conrad Ferdinand Meyers*. Europäische Hochschulschriften: Deutsche Literatur und Germanistik, series 1, 74. Bern: Herbert Lang, 1973.

Merton, Thomas. *Conjectures of a Guilty Bystander*. Garden City, New York: Image, 1968.

Meyer, Conrad Ferdinand. *Briefe Conrad Ferdinand Meyers nebst seinen*

Rezensionen und Aufsätzen. 2 vols. Edited by Adolf Frey. Leipzig: H. Haessel, 1908.

———. *The Complete Narrative Prose of Conrad Ferdinand Meyer.* 2 vols. Translated by George F. Folkers, David B. Dickens, and Marion W. Sonnenfeld. Lewisburg: Bucknell University Press, 1976.

———. *Sämtliche Werke. Historisch-kritische Ausgabe.* Vols. 11 and 12. Edited by Hans Zeller and Alfred Zäch. Bern: Benteli, 1959–61.

Molière. *Le Malade imaginaire.* Edited by Everett Ward Olmsted. New York: Ginn, 1905.

Moos, Carlo. *Dasein als Erinnerung: Conrad Ferdinand Meyer und die Geschichte.* Geist und Werk der Zeiten, 35. Edited by Rudolf von Albertini et al. Bern: Herbert Lang, 1973.

Nommensen, Ipke. *Erläuterungen zu Conrad Ferdinand Meyers* Das Amulett. 7th rev. ed. Erläuterungen zu den Klassikern, 273. Hollfeld/Obfr.: C. Bange, 1958.

Novalis. *Werke.* 3d ed. Hamburg: Hoffmann & Campe, 1966.

Øhrgaard, Per. *C. F. Meyer: Zur Entwicklung seiner Thematik.* Det Kongelige Danske Videnskabernes Selskab, Historisk-filosofiske Meddelelser 43, 2. Copenhagen: Munksgaard, 1969.

Onderdelinden, Sjaak. *Die Rahmenerzählungen Conrad Ferdinand Meyers.* Germanistisch-anglistische Reihe der Universität Leiden, 13. Edited by C. Soeteman, A. G. H. Bachrach, and J. G. Kooij. Leiden: Universitaire pers Leiden, 1974.

Reinhardt, George W. "On G. Lukács' Critique of C. F. Meyer: How is History Made?" *Colloquia Germanica* 15 (1982): 287–304.

———. "The Political Views of the Young Conrad Ferdinand Meyer with a Note on *Das Amulett.*" *German Quarterly* 45 (1972): 270–94.

———. "Two Romance Wordplays in C. F. Meyer's *Novellen.*" *Germanic Review* 46 (1971): 43–62.

Rippere, Victoria L. "Ludwig Tieck's 'Der blonde Eckbert': A Psychological Reading," *PMLA* 85 (1970); 473–86.

Ross, Nancy Wilson, ed. *The World of Zen: An East-West Anthology.* New York: Random House, 1960.

Rousseau. *The Confessions of Jean-Jacques Rousseau.* Translated by J. M. Cohen. New York: Penguin, 1982.

Sand, Christian. *Anomie und Identität: Zur Wirklichkeitsproblematik in der Prosa von C. F. Meyer.* Stuttgarter Arbeiten zur Germanistik, 79. Edited by Ulrich Müller, Franz Hundsnurscher, and Cornelius Sommer. Stuttgart: Hans-Dieter Heinz, 1980.

Schimmelpfennig, Paul. "C. F. Meyer's Religion of the Heart: A Reevaluation of *Das Amulett.*" *Germanic Review* 47 (1972): 181–202.

Schlegel, August Wilhelm. *Schriften.* Munich: Goldmann, n.d.

Shaw, Margaret R. B. Introduction to *Scarlet and Black,* by Stendhal. Baltimore: Penguin, 1969.

Shaw, Michael. "C. F. Meyer's Resolute Heroes: A Study of Becket, Astorre and Pescara." *Deutsche Vierteljahrschrift* 40 (1966): 360–90.

Sulloway, Frank J. *Freud, Biologist of the Mind: Beyond the Psychoanalytic Legend.* New York: Basic Books, 1979.

Swales, Martin. "Fagon's Defeat: Some Remarks on C. F. Meyer's *Das Leiden eines Knaben.*" *Germanic Review* 52 (1977): 29–43.

Tart, Charles T. "Out-of-the-Body Experiences." In *Psychic Exploration,* edited by E. Mitchell and J. White, pp. 349–74. New York: Putnam, 1974.

———. *States of Consciousness.* New York: E. P. Dutton, 1975.

Wiesmann, Louis. *Conrad Ferdinand Meyer: Der Dichter des Todes und der Maske.* Baseler Studien zur deutschen Sprache und Literatur, 19. Bern: Francke, 1958.

———. "Nachwort." *Das Leiden eines Knaben,* by C. F. Meyer. Stuttgart: Reclam, 1966.

Williams, W. D. *The Stories of C. F. Meyer.* Oxford: Clarendon, 1962.

Wyzewa, T. de. "Un romancier suisse, Conrad Ferdinand Meyer." *Revue des deux Mondes* 152 (1899): 934–45.

Zäch, Alfred. *Conrad Ferdinand Meyer: Dichtkunst als Befreiung aus Lebenshemmnissen.* Frauenfeld: Huber, 1973.

Index

monic force, 74–76; as descriptive term, 73; in the history of ideas, 64–76; and language, 67; philosophical view of, 64–67; as psychological phenomenon, 14, 21, 34–38, 40, 41, 46–48, 51–55, 57–61, 63–76, 107

Unconsciousness: and history, 12, 14, 20, 23–29, 70–71; as human condition (*see* Consciousness: egoic)

Unio mystica, 91

Unmasking trend, 71–72, 76

Vischer, Friedrich Theodor, 64, 71; *Kritische Gänge*, 64

Wagner, Richard, 73

Wallenstein, General von *(Gustav Adolfs Page)*, 52–54

War and Peace (Tolstoy), 25

Welt als Wille und Vorstellung, Die (Schopenhauer), 65

Will, 65, 66

Wonder, 87

World view, 63–64

Zen, 91, 92

Zwischen Himmel und Erde (Ludwig), 72